THE ULTIMATE POSITIVE AFFIRMATIONS GUIDE

Easily Attract And Achieve Success, Wealth, Health, Love, Self-Esteem, Happiness, Abundance and More

Dr. Stem
Helping Other People Excel

DR. STEM SITHEMBILE MAHLATINI

1

THE
ULTIMATE
POSITIVE
AFFIRMATIONS
GUIDE

Easily Attract And Achieve Success,
Wealth, Health, Love, Self-Esteem, Happiness,
Abundance and More

Written by: Dr. Stem Sithembile Mahlatini
Drstem14@gmail.com | www.drstemspeaks.com
https://www.drstemmie.com/
Facebook: DrStem Mahlatini Twitter: DrStemahlatini
LinkedIn: Drstem Mahlatini Skype: Dr.Mahlatini

Foreword by: Dr.Stem Sithembile Mahlatini
Cover Design by: Masimba Mukundinashe.

Category: Category: Journal, Journaling, Notebooks & Writing Pads, Diary, Motivational, Inspirational, Educational and Empowerment

Printed in the USA

My Mission for this book

1. To help you improve your life and achieve your goals. To provide you   with tools using Power Affirmations that you can begin using immediately to improve your life and help you achieve your goals. I especially want to help you achieve goals that can be measured like a specific increase in your relationships, lifestyle, and wealth.

2. To join with like-minded people who have used affirmations to change their lives and wellbeing. To make you a champion for change so that you too can teach others what you learned in this book.

Terms and Conditions

LEGAL NOTICE

THE ULTIMATE POSITIVE AFFIRMATIONS GUIDE

Easily Attract And Achieve Success, Wealth, Health, Love, Self-Esteem, Happiness, Abundance and More

Foreword

In practical advice books, like anything else in life, there are no guarantees in information in this book. The information is for educational purposes only.

This book is not intended for use as a source of mental health treatment, medical, legal, business, accounting, or financial advice. All readers are advised to seek services of competent professionals in mental, medical, legal, business, accounting, and finance fields.

Introduction

What do you desire most in life?

- To condition your mind to attract more money?
- More self-confidence, power and certainty?
- To create and maintain a peak state that will help you be more effective in everything you do? Hint: A peak state is different and much more powerful than just a positive attitude.
- Reduced debt?
- Weight loss?
- More friends?
- Peace of mind?
- More time with your family and friends (both quantity and quality)?
- Increased sales?
- A new home?
- Unlimited Funds in your bank account?
- Ability to help others financially.

What do you want specifically? Whatever it is, you already have within you the power to achieve these goals faster than you may currently believe is possible.

All you need to do is learn to unleash the massive power that lies within your own mind and focus it relentlessly on the results you want. Focus your mind and the results will follow: cause and effect. Sounds soooo simple, doesn't it? The answer is to put yourself into your personal peak state and condition yourself to stay there consistently.

Well, this is where most people run into challenges. Many never learn how to put themselves into a peak state on purpose in the first place. It may happen once in a while, and they feel great when it does, but then they don't learn how to get back into this state.

The other challenge is that they allow themselves to get knocked out of state or get discouraged. Or get stopped by fear. Their personal power disappears before they build enough momentum to make solid progress towards their desired goals. They let their minds wander aimlessly from thought to thought overly influenced by their environment

Dr. Stem
Helping Other People Excel

CONTENTS

Those who contemplate
the beauty of the earth
find reserves of strength
that will endure
as long as life lasts

Dr. Stem
Be Encouraged

Understanding
Affirmations

The Mystery of Human Existence lies not in just staying alive, but in finding something to live for

— Fyodor Dostoyevsky

What Are Affirmations?

Research has demonstrated that we have between 45,000 and 51,000 thoughts a day. That's about 150 to 300 thoughts a moment. Research has likewise demonstrated that for most individuals 80% of those thoughts are damaging. I wrote this book, with these results in mind. My focus is on us making that 80% turn to helpful thoughts than damaging thoughts.

My favorite part about manifesting your dream life is creating and saying positive statements that can help you keep your mind and energy affirmations, positive while you manifest your dreams.

Affirmations, truly, are simple, because it is all about being in conscious consistent command of your thoughts. Affirmations are brief, mighty positive uplifting statements. If you say them or think them or even hear them, they get to be the thoughts that produce your reality. In essence, positive affirmations are positively framed statements that are spoken in present tense about who you want to be and what you want in your life.

For example, let's say that I'm bad at managing money. I know that I want to become a good money manager, however, I need to change my belief that I'm bad at managing money. To start this process of change, I would begin telling myself that "I am a fast learner on good money management".

By verbalizing this phrase, consciously thinking about, and repeating it to myself regularly I will ultimately start to believe it be true – that I actually am a fast learner on good money management.

When I start to actually believe that I am a fast learner on good money management I then take action towards becoming a good money manager. Ultimately, I BECOME a fast learner on good money management.

The Basics Of Affirmations

Affirmations in reality make your sub-conscious thoughts conscious. Affirmations make you consciously cognizant of your thoughts. If you begin making conscious favorable thoughts, you in reality become more aware of the damaging thoughts that are constantly threatening to take over. You begin to affirm yourself and not compare yourself, your life with others in a discouraging way. The focus becomes manifesting, creating more and better, peace, joy, happiness, life, relationships and more.

Affirmations is an interesting phenomenon, in truth. It in reality proves true what your mother always cautioned: be careful of what you think as what you think is what you get.

She was essentially telling you that you produce what you think about, all the time.

When you're not cognizant of your thoughts, they tend to be damaging. And not being aware of your thoughts tends to induce an awful spiral downward, ultimately leading you to crushing down with sadness, depression, anxiety, low self-worth, fearful, etc.

Here is some truth that you might not know. Whatever you're thinking about, 90% gets carried forward to the next day's 51,000 thoughts. So, if you're thinking damaging thoughts, you'll cause yourself to think more damaging thoughts. This is not going to get you out of your mess, it continues to spiral.

Affirmations may change all of that! Affirmations make you conscious of your thoughts. To affirm means to state something positively. It means to announce firmly and assert something to be true. Affirmations are statements where you assert that what you wish to be real is real.

Here are a few affirmations examples of what you see more of in this book:
- I'm a success in all that I do
- I feel pleased, I feel healthy, I feel fantastic
- Everything feels just so correct
- I'm a money mogul
- My mind is clear centered and energized

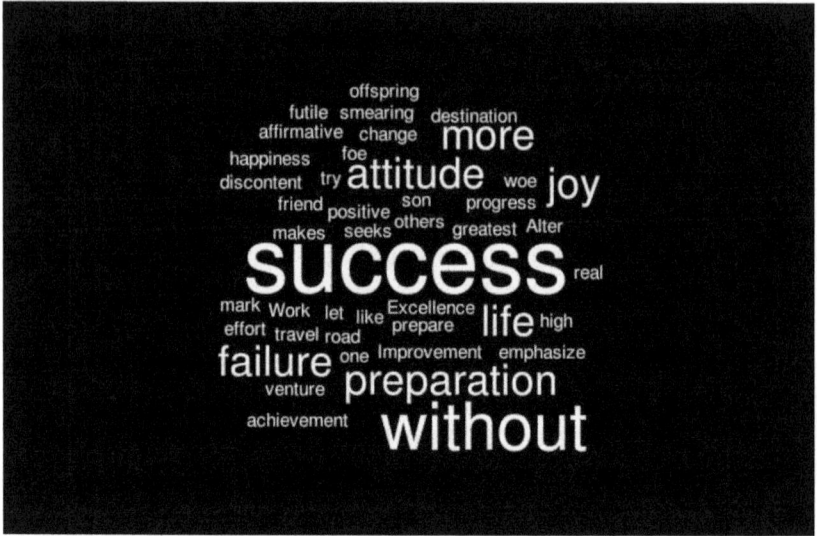

offspring
futile smearing destination
affirmative change more
happiness foe
discontent try attitude woe joy
friend positive son progress
makes seeks others greatest Alter
success real
mark Work let like Excellence life high
effort travel road prepare
failure one Improvement emphasize
venture preparation
achievement without

Over time affirmations overwrite any limiting or damaging beliefs and thoughts you might have about yourself or about not being able to do something, and substitute them with favorable thoughts and beliefs which instill self-confidence, belief, positivity, ambitiousness and much more.

Somebody who is perhaps a bit shy or un-confident would repeat affirmations about being confident. They would want to change themselves from being timid and introverted to becoming self-assured and more outgoing perhaps, and so they'd utilize favorable affirmations and repeat them again and again. And eventually they'd begin to sink in - the repetitive, favorable self-talk would begin to become a self-fulfilling prophecy. You are able to use the power of positive repetition for yourself at any time!

Utilizing favorable affirmations gives you back command of your mind and the information it gets. It puts you in the driver's seat of your brain and lets you flood it with favorable information which will change you for the better!

How Affirmations Make The Difference

What is the difference that makes the difference? Why do some people succeed where others fail? Why are there times when we feel unstoppable--in our power? And why are there times when we fail miserably?

Well, there are many explanations, but the one factor that seems to be consistent is that when we succeed, we enter our peak state. This is a mental state of mind where anything that is possible becomes possible for us. All our resources become immediately available. People are attracted to us automatically. Where we are better than our best. Where we are in the zone. If you have been in this state even once in your life, you know what I'm talking about.

Affirmative prayers

This part is for my fellow believers out there.

As one who grew up in church, it took me a while to understand affirmative prayer. I thought praying was

telling God about my problems and begging for his divine answers in every prayer. I now know different; it is not so.

Affirmative prayer is a sort of prayer or a metaphysical process that's centered on a favorable outcome instead of a negative situation. For instance, an individual who is experiencing some form of illness would focus the prayer on the wanted state of perfect health and affirm this desired intention "as if already occurred" instead of identifying the illness and then asking The Higher Power for help to do away with it. So when praying one prays for healing, reads about healing and see themselves healed.

Many a time I struggled with prayers and sermons that are focused on the illness, the troubles, the lack. Now I know why. I was overwhelmed with the need to focus on problems and celebrating the moment and the answers to come, so that we can live in the joy of knowing and trusting God will make all things work together for our good.

Once I learned that it is better and healthier to celebrate each moment, each day and focus on his answers, I noticed that I felt better, I did better, and I believed more when my prayers were focused on what God Promised for my life, when I prayed and focused on possibilities than on my fears and difficulties, my whole outlook and prayers changed.

The Benefits of Affirmations

Repeating daily affirmations isn't just a "feel good" exercise for making you more positive and optimistic. Affirmations have some real benefits including:

- They reinforce your goals and help you achieve them.
- They motivate you to take positive, forward-moving action in your daily activities.
- They allow you to focus more on positive thoughts than self-defeating thoughts.
- They help relieve stress and anxiety.
- They foster mental clarity and focus.
- They help build stronger, more intimate relationships.
- They improve feelings of gratitude, appreciation, and general happiness.
- They work in tandem with other mindfulness activities like meditation and present moment awareness.

The Concept Behind
Affirmations

*Dreams are extremely important. You can't do it
unless you can imagine it.*

——————————————————————— George Lucas

Wish Prosperity Manifestation Dream
Expansion
Feeling Abundance Focus Resonance
Health
Creation The Law of Wealth
Love Joy
Attraction
Intention Consciousness
Expansion Happy
Soul Awareness Receive
Attention Attitude

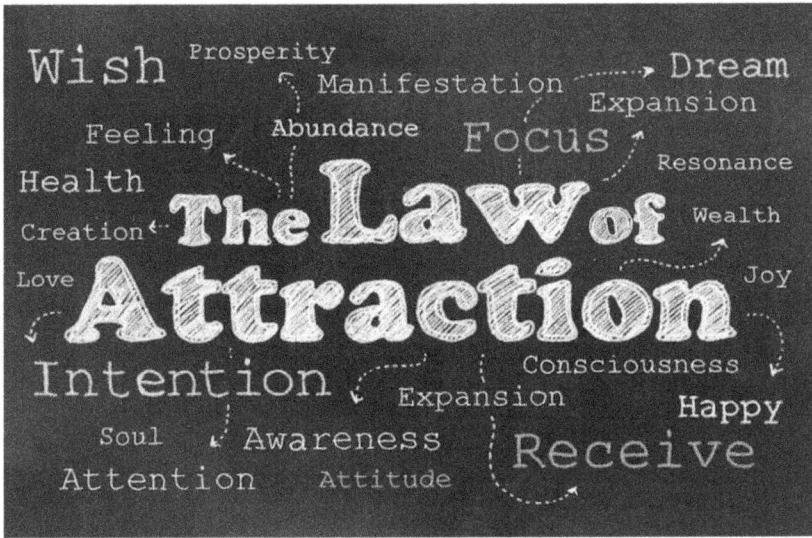

The Law Of Attraction

For those who know me, I have been studying the law of attraction for years, teaching and practicing it.

It is one way I can inspire, encourage, and empower others to change their lives and achieve more.

If you could change your frequency, you could change your life. If you could change your vibration, you could change your life. If you could get rid of negativity, fear, resentment, unforgiveness you could change your life.

Why is it that we duplicate patterns and draw the same sort of friends or lovers? Some individuals think that we give out a vibration that magnetically draws in others on a like vibration.

Our vibration is neutral – it doesn't understand what is good or bad for us so if we believe all men are traitorous, all jobs lead nowhere or we'll constantly be poor, we may attract those experiences. The media is forever flooding us with fear and bad news altogether out of proportion to reality.

How may we make a shift to get our minds to trust in the positive?

Consciously practice being non-judgmental and compassionate. Be cognizant and always aware of your inner dialogue. If somebody succeeds or wins what is your response? Embrace the uniqueness in other people and viewpoints. Don't take things personally.

It's crucial to be aware of the energy you put out, as it is like a calling signal or lighthouse drawing in the same vibration back. If you get jealous or mad, if you're petty or judgmental, it's likely that you'll call in others who mimic this energy. We frequently have different rules for ourselves than other people.

Being in nature is an excellent way of becoming clear about your desires. In the stillness of nature, or ocean front are places that work for me. Practice and enjoy knowing your ability to cosmically order grows with each success.
Ask and You will Receive.
Act and Sow, You will Reap

Introduction to Cosmic Ordering

Your cosmic order will only be accomplished if you really feel you deserve it. The old adage that if you don't love yourself how may anybody else love you is right. Love yourself and trust you deserve it and the universe ought to put your order at the top.

A central point to remember is that we'll only get 'what we trust is conceivable' if you don't trust your order is possible, it has less chance of occurring. To trust you'll sprout wings and fly is obviously not going to occur, as your inner consciousness won't believe it's possible. Some individuals could never believe they'll win the lottery, yet do it ever week without fail. Uhmmm I always wonder, why, why, why. Someplace inside them there's a block and therefore it will never become truth.

My belief is that if you trust you deserve it and, crucially, believe it's conceivable, then it may happen. But, it's crucial to listen to your inner guide. There's no point ordering things you don't trust may happen as, by centering on your orders not happening, you're in effect wiping out your order!

So begin by ordering things you do think may happen and, when you get the hang of it, aim higher.

How Do Positive Affirmations Work?

Mahatma Gandhi has a famous quote that outlines how your beliefs shape your destiny. He is quoted as saying:

> *"Your beliefs become your thoughts,*
> *Your thoughts become your words,*
> *Your words become your actions,*
> *Your actions become your habits,*
> *Your habits become your values,*
> *Your values become your destiny."*

So, what exactly are we changing when we say positive affirmations?

Effectively, we're changing our thinking and our beliefs, which, in turn, will create behavioral change and improved results. The thing is there's no magic pill. Changing a belief can be hard if it is well engrained in our mind.

All of your thoughts, feelings, experiences, and results throughout your whole life have led you to believe certain things to be true. With all of this "evidence" backing up your belief, no wonder changing a belief is hard!

However, there is a specific technique to **saying positive affirmations that will help you get the results you desire.**

When Do I Say Positive Affirmations? I am glad you asked.

Positive affirmations are not something that you simply say once off and expect to see massive improvements. If you want to build confidence, saying to yourself "I am confident" once won't create any lasting change. It may give you that little bit of extra confidence to overcome an immediate hurdle, however I'm here to help you make long-lasting change that you embody in your everyday life – eventually, without even thinking about it.

Therefore it's important that you commit to making positive affirmations part of your everyday routine. It needs to become habit and needs to become automatic.

Let's talk about some good times to say positive affirmations.

1. Morning Routine

Do you have a morning routine? If not, you should have one.

The most productive people I know have a specific morning routine they follow every day. I've recently been focused on implementing a solid morning routine and I'm seeing some amazing results in terms of overall wellbeing and productivity each day.

As part of your morning routine, say some positive affirmations to get your mindset and belief system working for you each day.

For example, in the morning when I first wake up I lie in bed, take 5 mindful deep breaths, visualize the day I have planned for myself and say the positive affirmation "This is going to be an Amazing Day under grace in divine order. Today I am going to be super-productive".

By saying positive affirmations as part of your morning routine you can be certain that you'll be saying them regularly and it will be much more likely to become a habit.

2. During a Regular Activity

You can say your affirmations during the following regular daily activities:

- Every morning on your way to work
- Having lunch
- Before you enter a room for a meeting
- Before you open the door at home each evening
- Brushing your teeth
- Going to the bathroom, in the bathroom
- ... just to name a few places

Again, using these regular moments will help you create the habit of saying these positive affirmations and over time they will become natural and you'll think of them outside of these regular moments.

3. During a Specific but Important or Challenging Activity

Perhaps there are activities that you only do on certain days or perhaps it's less frequent such as once a week or once a fortnight.

These activities are often challenging. But they are important, and you want to make sure you are performing at your best during these times. It's times like this where you need to get focused and be your best self.

Examples might be:
- Getting on stage to present
- Going on a date
- Leading a meeting
- Picking up the phone to prospect

Just before each of these activities, you can say 1 to 3 affirmations that will reinforce the belief that you are creating. The simple fact of being about to perform these activities will remind you to say your positive affirmations.

For example, if I'm about to present a workshop I would say to myself "I love facilitating. This is what I do best" and "I was born to do this". Even at times when I'm feeling unprepared or extremely nervous, I would say these positive affirmations and they would help refocus my thoughts and therefore how I perform during the session.

4. Ad-hoc or Spontaneous Challenges

Sometimes there are challenges that suddenly come up in our lives. Perhaps it's your boss that comes and tells you that she needs a report completed and sent to her within the next 2 hours and you know you're already struggling for time. Or perhaps it's that bump into an ex-lover who broke your heart.

In these situations, you can quickly turn to a positive affirmation to help you get in the right mindset. For example, if your boss asks for a report due immediately that you can't say no to, you might say "I am a great problem-solver, I think outside the box" or "I love these challenges, this is going to be a great test of my ability.

Let's do it!"

30

You can also use in the case of bumping into an ex-lover who broke your heart you might say something like "I forgive her" or "I'm excited to catch up".

In these situations, you may not have embodied specific beliefs because you haven't been stating these affirmations on a regular basis, but you can take a moment to frame the situation in the positive which effectively does the same thing, but just for the immediate term. It's just a matter of being conscious of your thoughts.

How to Say a Positive Affirmation

Simply saying the words of a positive affirmation is not going to have any significant effect on your life. **You need to FEEL it.** It's about embodying what you're saying.

It's a hard thing to describe, but you want to physiologically get your mind and body to truly believe in the statement that you're saying. For example, stating "I am super confident" while internally thinking "I sound like an idiot. I don't believe this. What am I doing?" is not going to get you anywhere. That is going to be counter-productive.

Instead, when stating "I am super confident" you want to stand like a confident person would stand. You want to sound like a confident person would sound. You want to breathe like a confident person would breathe. You want to visualize yourself as a confident person.

See the difference?

THAT'S the secret of positive affirmations.

The secret is physiologically experiencing what you want to experience.

Remember, it's a self-perpetuating cycle. When you think and feel it, you will behave differently, you will see different results and ultimately your core beliefs will naturally be shaped over time to the point you no longer even need those positive affirmations. You simply ARE those beliefs.

Simple Steps to Saying Positive Affirmations

If this is your first time trying the power of positive affirmations, do these steps (i.e., DO IT NOW... it takes 10 seconds):

Take a deep breath

Say IT.. say your positive affirmation. As you're saying the positive affirmation, ALSO do the below

VISUALIZE .. visualize yourself as how you want to be (eg confident. Create vivid imagery in your mind about what you are confident doing). If it's easier, close your eyes.

FEEL IT...feel how you want to feel by stating that positive affirmation (eg confident).

SPEAK IT...speak how you would when living that affirmation (eg confident).

Take a moment to think about how good you feel.

That's it!

Positive affirmations are simple!

But just remember the two secret components to make them effective: Physiologically experience the positive affirmation

Say your affirmations regularly

I hope by reading this book, you feel empowered to change any negative thought patterns you may have fallen into. We're all human and it's not possible to be positive or optimistic all the time, but you always have the power to make huge changes in your life by simply reframing your thoughts.

Manifesting Your Dream Life

Before you dive into creating or writing about your Dream Life affirmations let me ask you a few questions, actually a lot of insightful questions.

Do you ever feel like...

- Your source of internal energy is running dangerously low?

- You're daydreaming your life away with fantasies of... more—but maybe you aren't quite sure what that is?

- Your family is simply existing in the same household, but you don't feel connected?

- Your household is a never-ending spew of stuff-to-do?

- You forget birthdays, you don't text back, or you're stuck in a "we should make plans soon!" circle of friendship hell?

- You're struggling to connect with your partner or your relationship isn't where you think it should be?

- You've lost control over your body or you don't feel comfortable in your own skin?

- It feels like forever since you went on an adventure or did something fresh and exciting?

- Your job or business is feeling lackluster or repetitive, boring or burning you out?

- There's never enough money to do all the things you want to do (or buy all the things you want to buy)?

- Your dream life feels like way more of a dream than a reality?

If you answered even one of the above Yeah? Then you're in the right place. It is time to make changes. Before we begin, let's have a quick talk. What is a "Dream Life" anyway? Maybe for you, it means having a housekeeper who keeps the dishes in your sink sparkling clean (and your laundry perfectly folded).

Maybe it means having enough time for your varied creative pursuits as well as building a booming business. Or maybe its means a swanky house, flashy car and/or exotic family vacations every summer (or every few weeks!).

The truth?

It could be all of these things, or something else entirely. Everybody's dream life is different, which is exactly why it's so important to take some time to regularly reflect on what it is we truly want (and not what society tells us we should want, or our best friends or biz besties want, or what our parents or partner desperately wish we wanted).

There's truly only one big difference between people who are living their dream lives, and those who continue to only daydream about a better future. That difference? Clarity. And that's exactly what this journal was designed to help you achieve.

By the way: If you're new to journaling, it might feel daunting, or frivolous or even silly. But it's truly an incredibly powerful manifestation tool—and it's literally right at our fingertips all the time! While that doesn't mean you can write on paper that you want a new car and a Ferrari will instantly & magically park itself in your garage. But what journaling does do is provide you with a tool to take those pie-in-the-sky fantasies out of your head, put them on paper, set your intentions and start actively working toward them.

One thing I know is that if you don't gain clarity on your dream life, you'll never turn it into reality. Even small, incremental steps can make a huge difference over time.

If you're ready to cut through confusion & finally figure out what you truly desire, then let's put your dream life on paper.
On my website www.drstemmie.com I have a FREE webinar on Journaling that has helped many understand the Power of Journaling. Visit the site to see the webinar.

Don't be a parrot in life, **be an eagle.** A parrot talks way too much but can't fly high but an eagle is silent and has the will power to

Touch the Sky

- Unknown Author

The Mindset for Affirmations

Failure is the opportunity to begin again, this time more intelligently than before.

— Henry Ford

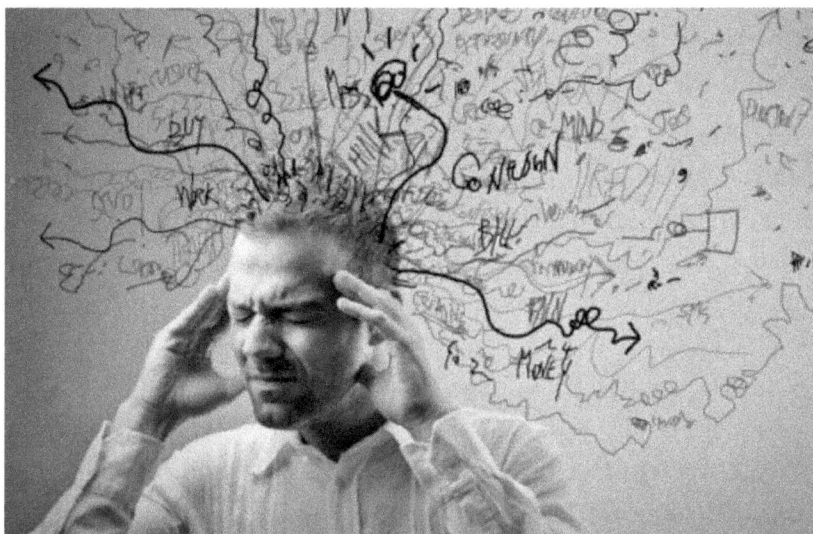

The Battle For Your Mind And Mindset Shifts

Think about this. How do advertisers influence us to spend billions of dollars on the products they sell? The answer is contained in the question itself: advertisers advertise. They Repeatedly, Relentlessly advertise. Through TV and radio commercials, magazine ads, billboards, etc. And they do it more by influencing your emotional states than by logical arguments.

A major company with a multimillion-dollar advertising budget will use all these means to fight for a permanent piece of your brain. We have become so conditioned to the media blitz around us that we hardly pay attention anymore. It just feels natural.

And then there are demands for our attention by other people. Well-meaning family members and friends. Our employers. Civic groups. Politicians.The news. Social Media. When you think about it, there's so much noise in most of our environments (including non-verbal "noise") it's no wonder that we find it difficult to stay focused on our own goals.

How Do We Take Back Control?

Well, one method that I have tried is reading and/or listening to self-help materials. Over the years, such materials have helped me and millions of others transform our lives. The world owes a huge debt to the authors and publishers of these materials, over and over.

But self-help materials have also proven a challenge. Who has time to read or listen to all of it? And even when I have time to read or listen, who the heck can remember all the critical points? To maximize my time, I do most of my listening in my car, however this means that taking notes is almost impossible at times.

Here's a simple test for you. Think back to a book or audio program that has had a profound, positive influence on your life. Now take out a piece of paper and make a list of the 10 most important points from the material **from memory.** If you can't remember 10, can you remember 5? Now how well can you **really** explain these points? Hard right?

Here's the BIG question: how often do you **APPLY** these ideas in your everyday life? Unless you are an exceptional person--or unless you have really studied the material through repeated readings/listenings (and took notes) my guess is that you didn't remember a lot of specifics. It's more of just a "feeling" about the book. Or maybe a single powerful idea that changed the entire course of your thinking (usually by putting you into a temporary peak state).

Now if I say to you "Just Do It" "Designed for Driving Pleasure" "America Runs on Dunkin" I'll bet most of you can name the company or products that I'm referring to. Why? Because advertisers have used print, radio, and television advertisements to present these slogans to us over and over and over again.

And they mix their appeals with the emotions of sex, beauty, power, prestige, laughter--or they make us feel fear by not using their product. And they send the same messages through different media enhanced by music and pictures. For some "unknown" reason, we end up spending **billions** of dollars for their products. **Logic** smells, **emotion sells.**

"Advertise" to Your Own Mind

Get the idea? I hope you do. If you want to have control of your own mind, you are going to have to fight for it. This is the reason that I founded The Empowerment Academy, with self-help programs to help empower, encourage, and educate personal and professional development programs which include the power of affirmations.

Mindset Shifts To Enhance Your Affirmations

Your mindset plays a huge part in how you view yourself and the world. With thousands of thoughts floating around in your head every day, you essentially talk to yourself more than anybody else.

The mind houses our emotions, judgments, worries, and secrets, and many of us don't even realize that our own thoughts can be holding us back from reaching our full potential.

Because the mind is such a powerful place, it's important to constantly grow and adapt your ways of thinking. You have to continuously work on shifting your mindset to embrace new perspectives if you want to become a more accepting person.

In this book, I'm sharing some ways that I've adapted and shifted my mindset over the years to improve my life in a positive way. Keep in mind that I too have had to use these affirmations and seen the power and impact affirmation can have on life, love, business, career, or relationships.

There are however very, very few moments when I do none of the following and wallow in self-pity, but I can usually pick myself up from a bad situation and turn it around with the help of these mindset shifts. Remember I said very few twice, because when you know better, you do better, when you learn you grow.

Let's get into shifting your mindset to get you ready to practice affirmations that will work miracles in your life as well. I am excited to hear or read about your testimonials.

Shift-1. Trusting that better things are coming

I'm very blessed that I'm naturally quite an optimistic person. No matter what happens to me, I've always been able to keep moving forward. Part of this is my belief that better things will always come to me if I work hard and don't give up.

When I was at a job that frustrated me on a daily basis, I found other ways to keep myself sane. I went for walks on my lunch breaks and listened to music or podcasts. I started a blog. I also made an effort to try harder at work so that I spent less time complaining about it.

I knew that I wasn't going to be there forever, and even though I was uncertain where I was going to end up, I knew I should try to find ways to make myself happy in the meantime. In the end, things fell into place and I was given the opportunity to create my dream job. Better things always come along if you're open to the possibilities.

Shift-2. Enjoying the process while working toward your goals.

Mindfulness is all about living in the present moment, but how do you focus on the present while you're busy working toward your goals for the future? It's an interesting paradox that I struggled with for a while. Over time, I realized that you could set goals for the future, but you have to be present and focused while you're working to accomplish them.

I used to always rush through projects just to get them "over with," but I realized that's not a good way to live my life. Instead, I told myself to enjoy the process a little bit more. When you're always rushing through things in order to move on to the next project, you miss opportunities to be creative and produce your best work.

These days, I try to be more present when I'm working on something. Reflection is important, so I've started doing weekly and monthly check-ins with myself to stop myself from charging ahead into the future.

Shift-3. Focusing on my strengths over my weaknesses

We all have our weaknesses and things that make us question our worthiness as humans. I know that I can be very critical of myself and delay doing what I believe in, encouraging others and coaching them to be great when I have so much to share and so much proof that what I do works. That was then, I am now on fire, want to birth all that has been brewing in me.

Self doubt occurs to many of us, it is normal as long you read my self-sabotage free eBOOK and learn how to get out of your own way, you will be good. Over the years, I've found that it's much more productive and beneficial to truly focus on leveling up my strengths than trying to overhaul all of my weaknesses. Though I may look like I am not doing anything, I am working on something most of the time. I do work really hard on the things I'm passionate about and now am not afraid to share it all, including this affirmations book.

Of course you should try to be a better person in every way that you can, but there are parts of you that you simply don't have to worry about so much about changing. Once I realized that I could focus my energy on taking my strengths to the next level instead of worrying about my weaknesses, my relationship with myself became a lot better.

Shift-4. Spend less time worrying about the past

I've come to genuinely accept that the past is the past and there's nothing I can do about it. I can speculate about how things might be different in my life if I'd have chosen to do things another way, but there is literally nothing productive about wishing I could change the past.

Sometimes I remind myself that even if I could go back in time and change things, there's no saying that it would alter my life or make me a happier person. All I can do is move forward and use past mistakes to drive me closer to a better future.

Shift 5. Optimizing what's in my control

No matter how much I think about it, I cannot control exactly what my future will look like but now I know that I can believe in all possibilities available to me. I'll admit that I spend more time thinking about the future than I do the past. I used to get anxious not knowing if all my dreams and vision board items would come to life before I die, yes, I worried a lot even though I spoke about my vision and would see clearly how that would be possible. I look back and I had nothing to worry about after all. I let go of worry and focused on preparing myself for this moment. I say to you never give up preparing for what you want, one day it will all come together.

It does. Dreams do come true.

Since there are actions, I can take right now, I try to focus my energy, thoughts, and time on doing those actions instead of worrying about the future.

I've learned that it's 100 times more productive to take action in the current moment than spend time overthinking what hasn't even happened yet.

The Practice & Discipline For Affirmations

Never let your work drive you. Master it and keep it in complete control.

— Booker T. Washington

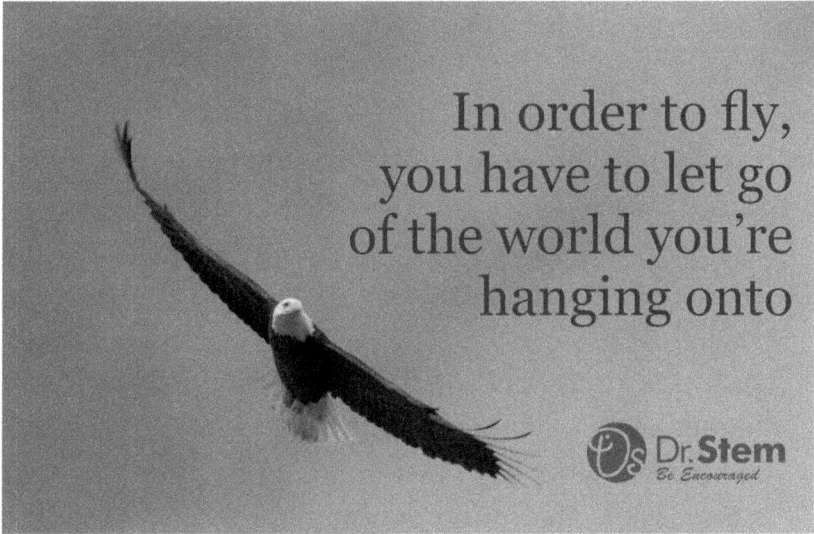

In order to fly,
you have to let go
of the world you're
hanging onto

Dr.Stem
Be Encouraged

How To Use Affirmations

Some people say affirmations out loud in front of a mirror. Others simply write them down in a journal. You can also repeat them in your head like a mantra during meditation.

The important thing is to find affirmations that resonate with you. I'll admit that there are plenty of affirmations I had to change to match what resonates with me many a time.

Some people have problems with saying words like "higher power", "universe", "manifest" and "abundance,". The words just don't resonate with them, and that's ok. Replace with words that resonate with you, and make it work. That is the key.

The important thing is to find affirmations that resonate with you.

What is the most effective way to use Power Affirmations?

Here are a few suggestions.

1. Pick one or two affirmations and begin using them immediately. Don't wait until you create the "perfect" affirmations for your specific situation before you start using them. The future is now. Procrastination is the killer of success. Immediate action creates Momentum. Repetition of positive thought Sustains it. Do not base your choice by whether you already believe the affirmation or if the belief seems possible to you at this time.

   Repeating the power affirmations with emotional intensity and a feeling of certainty will eventually install the beliefs in your subconscious mind. At the very least, pick a generic affirmation like "Every day in every way I'm getting better and better." Then you can always choose or create other power affirmations later after you set specific goals.

2. Write the power affirmation at least 10-20 times per day. For best results, write it down 10-20 times as soon as you arise and 10-20 times before you go to bed. This allows you to set the direction of your thoughts before

the day starts and plant the seed in your subconscious mind before you go to sleep. If you do this consistently, you will naturally find this thought re-occurring in your mind several times per day.

You will notice the power affirmations shaping your other thoughts through the course of the day. As the power affirmations create more and more similar thoughts, you will create a direction and build momentum towards the desired results.

3. After you write the affirmation 10-20 times, repeat it aloud in front of a mirror 5-10 times. Repeating the affirmations aloud further installs the beliefs into your subconscious mind. It is very important to repeatedly both write and audibly state your affirmations for maximum effectiveness.

4. As you write and audibly repeat them, feel the emotional power of the affirmations in your body. See yourself as having already created this result in your life. Feel the way you would feel if you already had this result in your life. Hear the things you will hear when this affirmation becomes an everyday reality. Breathe the way you would breathe if this affirmation were already true. Move your body as if this were already a conditioned belief.

5. Now let your positive thoughts of power and certainty guide your actions. Live consciously. Take complete

control of your own mind rather than passively allowing the influencers in the media control it for you.

6. Combine using the affirmations with a goal setting and daily progress measurement program. By measuring your progress daily, it is much easier to see where you are succeeding (and celebrate!) and see where you need to improve. Daily? Well, everyone is different, but that's what I've found necessary for myself.

Absolutely...daily because this is where most people fail. They don't follow through with these steps every day for a long period of time. They get inspired for a few days after hearing a motivational speaker or after reading a book. Then, after the motivational "high" wears off, they fall back into their old habits. Or they get so busy that this is an easy item to ignore. Successful people take the actions that unsuccessful people will not.

Event training through short seminars, etc. is necessary and great. But Process Training, training that guides your everyday habits, is the real key to sustained results.

Process Training is achieved through sustained exposure to the learning material over a prolonged period. And it requires constant review and correction until the skill is installed as a subconscious habit (like how you learn to drive a car). Most people who think they can get all the information they need by attending a couple of seminars or listening to a bestselling program one time will usually be disappointed. The information just goes by too fast to allow it to really soak in.

Why do you think we see the same commercials repeatedly? Or hear the same slogan? It's because advertisers know if they can get our attention for 30 seconds (or less), listen to or watch the same commercial multiple times over a period of days, weeks, months, years, they know they can sell us billions of dollars of merchandise. Isn't it time that you used the exact same technique to condition your mind on purpose? Take control of your mind.

Listening to motivational speakers on audio tape on a regular basis (in other words, daily) is one effective way to add process training to your life; however, many of the thoughts they communicate race by without having a chance to take root in either your conscious or subconscious mind. And there's often a lot of fluff just to get to the main points that will really change your life. It's much more difficult to take advantage of the power of repetition which is crucial to create long term results.

If you have not checked it out I do have audio inspirational/motivational books where I read the books myself and many people have said listening to them over and over has helped them shift and follow their heart. They are under empowerment ebooks.

All Birds find shelter during a rain. But Eagle avoids rain by flying above the Clouds.

Creating Your Own Power Affirmations

You don't have to use the affirmations on this site to achieve the results you want. You can easily create your own. Your only limit is your own limitless imagination.

Here are some guidelines to help you:

Keep them short. You will find in most cases that a single sentence is not only sufficient to state your belief, it is preferable. It reduces the time to repeat your affirmation, it also allows you to more easily remember your affirmation throughout the day.

Keep them positive. Say "I am now relaxed and have peace of mind," rather than "I have no stress." The problem with the last affirmation is that you have to think about what stress means to you in order to think about "no stress." And as you focus on what stress means to you, there is a greater possibility that you will actually create **more** stress.

If someone tells you "Don't picture an elephant," what happens? Power affirmations work by **consistently** controlling your focus so that you focus only on what you want, not on what you don't want.

Keep them in the present. Say "my physical power, energy, and vitality are now exploding massively," rather than "in three months I will have all the physical power, energy, and vitality I desire." A power affirmation is **not** always a statement of current "reality." That is not the purpose of using power affirmations.

The purpose of power affirmations is to **create** what you desire by transforming intangible invisible thought into physical reality. A reality that most likely does not presently exist in your life. Think about it. If what you were confessing already existed in your life, it wouldn't be necessary for you to use the affirmations.

As you use power affirmations, you are training your subconscious mind to direct your focus and your activities to **automatically** move you in the direction of the end result that you desire.

For example, even though you repeat the power affirmation "I am now wealthy," you probably don't have all the money you want or probably need in the moment. Your present reality may be that you are deeply in debt and struggling to make ends meet; however, by repeating this affirmation 10-20 times twice each day with emotional conviction and emotional energy, your mind will automatically begin looking for ways to create more wealth.

You will begin to see and take advantage of opportunities you didn't see before. You will read books on wealth that you didn't even know existed. You will develop new beliefs about what is possible.

Over time, these subtle changes in your everyday thinking will move you into the direction of creating more wealth. At the very least, you will create more wealth than you would have without using the power affirmation. Most likely, you will create more wealth than you may currently believe is possible. **The feeling of wealth actually creates more wealth.** This is one of the reasons why the "rich get richer." Power Affirmations used repeatedly help you to create a feeling of wealth before it actually exists in your life.

Ask yourself, **"What do I have to believe in order to achieve the results I want?"** And **"What are the *specific* results I desire?"** People who achieve outstanding results in a particular area think differently than people who achieve poor or average results in that area.

Be a beliefs detective.

When you make this an area of focus, you will be surprised at what you begin to notice as you read books, talk to others, watch TV and movies, etc. You will begin to see how people's beliefs and consistent focus created their current reality--both good and bad.

As you begin to detect the conscious and unconscious beliefs of others, you can select the ones that will create the reality that you desire and reject the beliefs that are preventing you from achieving the results you desire. Choose your beliefs.

Juice up the language of your power affirmations by adding words of positive emotional intensity.

The power of affirmations is multiplied when you add emotional conviction. For example, instead of saying "I am now creating all the wealth I want and need," say "My imagination is now creating the massive financial abundance that I need and desire."

Why do great athletes physically pump themselves up by chanting, yelling, jumping up and down, etc.? It's because it increases their energy and sharpens their minds. They psych themselves up to **feel** strong and powerful. While not a substitute for skill and ability (usually gained through repetition--practice), it helps them put forth their best effort and achieve superior results.

There are many other points I could make about power affirmations, but they are not as important as your beginning to **use them right away.** Only then you will begin to experience the benefits for yourself. Their power will become real to you and you will continue to use them for the rest of your life.

The next several chapters have the Power Affirmations that I have and continue to use for myself and assign to the patients and clients I have worked with in my work and a mental health professional, life, career and business coach and trainer.

These are tested in the trenches of personal experience. Use them regularly and they will work for you as they have for myself and many others.

Eye Opening Life Questions And Prompts

These eye-opening pprompts are designed to help you really understand what you want out of life, in every area from relationships to career to business and more.

Before we dive in, though, know this: It's okay and totally normal to feel resistance to some (or all!) of these prompts. Many of them are direct, pointed questions and you can take your time to answer them. - **Now, let's do this!**

Intellectual Growth

a) What does intellectual growth mean to you? In an ideal world, in what ways would you regularly expand your mind?

b) Let's dig a little deeper. What topics fascinated you as a child? Are you still curious about it? How could you infuse more of it into your life?

c) What kind of literature did you enjoy when you were younger? Are there any unread books sitting on your shelf you'd love to devour?

d) What would you love to spend more time learning about if you had "all the time in the world"?

e) Morbid, but useful: Is there anything you'd regret not learning if you were toward the end of your life? A new language, getting your PhD in physics, or becoming a certified coach, for example?

f) List the top 5 things you want to learn/know in the next 5 years. You can start with your answer above, and then add more.

Spiritual Growth

a) What does spiritual growth look like to you? Does it involve connecting with a higher self, a higher entity or the Universe at large?

b) What spiritual practices do you wish you had more time for? In a perfect world, what spiritual practices would you engage in on a daily basis? How about a weekly, monthly or yearly basis?

c) What role would spirituality play in your life in your dream life? A small role? A big one?

d) What spiritual goals would you love to achieve in your

life? Would you learn to trust your intuition, do shadow work or pray on the daily?

e) What does your spirituality/spiritual practice look like in your dream life? Describe tangibly what engaging in "spirituality" looks like in your ideal future. Do you attend a religious service? Do you have an altar space in your home?

f) What do you want to learn about when it comes to spirituality? What would you know about or be able to do or have in your dream life when it comes to spirituality? (Example: "I'd have studied yoga, and be working with a Reiki master," or "I'd feel more connected to God everyday." Remember: There are no wrong answers!)

Family

a) In your dream life, what does your family look like? Who is a part of your family? List everybody from immediate family members to the other family you are ideally connected to.

b) How do you interact and connect with your family in your dream life?

c) What rituals do you and your family have in your dream life? (Do you always eat meals together? Do you have "Self Care Sundays" with your daughter every week?)

d) Are there any relationships with family members you'd change in your dream life? If so, who is involved and how would you ideally like it to change?

e) What are the things that define you as a family in your ideal world? What makes your family special? Are you honest and open with one another? Are you close? Do you have inside jokes?

f) What makes your ideal family life different than your current family life? What would need to change to get closer to the ideal?

House & Home

a) What does your ultimate living situation look like? What do you envision for your house and/or home and living situation? Do you live in a large home? An apartment? An RV?

b) In your dream life, where do you live? You can get specific by naming an actual place, or simply something like, "the beach."

c) What does it look like? What physical features are included in your dream home (a big garden, a jacuzzi tub, a walk-in closet)? Write about the ULTIMATE space you'd feel most comfortable, safe, and excited to live in.

d) Who do you live with in an ideal world? What do they do to contribute to the overall sense of "home" in your house?

e) Let's talk aesthetics. Is your dream home full of sentimental items? Is it minimalist? Do you have an ideal aesthetic? If so, describe it with a few adjectives, or go deeper if you'd like.

f) How do you feel in your home? How do you want others to feel in your home?

g) How do you feel in your bedroom, specifically? Does it feel conducive to peace, relaxation and sleep? What does it look like? What makes it so great? Could you expand the energy of that room into the rest of the house? What would that look like?

h) What do you use your home for? Work? Play? Both? How does what's in your home support that?

i) How often do you have others to your home? Or do you not have others in your home?

j) Do you own more than one home or call more than one place home? If so, where are your other homes?

Friendships & Social Life

a) What does your ideal social life look like?

b) Are you introverted or extroverted? Do you prefer socializing in small groups or one-on-one? Are you always invited to the biggest, most extravagant parties, or do you prefer more intimate conversations?

c) How do you FEEL around your closest friends? What are they like? Why do you love them so much?

d) What things do you do with your friends? Do you have any shared activities or interests?

e) How do you keep in touch? How often do you see your friends? What do you do together?

f) What kind of friend are you? What qualities do you have? How do your friends describe you, in your dream life?

g) Is there anyone specifically you'd like to be closer to and you imagine as your "inner circle" in your dream life?

h) What qualities do your "dream" friends have? What friends that are currently in your life already meet these standards/have these qualities?

Romantic Relationships

a) In your dream life, who is your IDEAL partner? Is it someone you already know (like a current partner), or someone you've yet to meet?

b) What does your dream partner look like?

c) How does your dream partner make you feel?

d) What are the non-negotiable in your dream relationship? What behaviors do you expect? What behaviors do you not tolerate?

e) How does your dream partner treat you? What does s/he do for you? How does s/he speak to you?

f) What does your time with your partner look like? What types of activities and dates do you go on together? Be as wild and imaginative as you like (bring on the hot air balloon rides)!

g) How does your partner show you love in the ways that are important to you?

h) List 5 traits that are absolute must-haves in your dream partner.

i) List 5 traits that are absolute must-haves in your dream relationship.

Health & Fitness

a) Your body isn't everything—but it is an incredible tool that allows you to live out your dream life. In your dream life, what does your body LOOK like?

b) How do you feel IN your body? Do you feel strong, sexy, light?

c) How do you feel ABOUT your body?

d) How do you nourish your body? What foods do you consume? How do you feel after each meal?

e) How do you keep yourself fit and healthy? What types of movement do you engage in and how often?

f) What other self care activities do you do that contribute to your overall wellness?

g) What health and/or fitness activities do you engage in everyday? (Example: Do you meditate every morning or go on an evening walk after dinner each night? Do you cook your dinners—or do you have a chef?)

Adventures & Experiences

a) Humans are curious, adventurous beings. What types of adventure do you engage in in your ideal life? Is it climbing up mountains, trying out new restaurants or playing fantasy video games? All of the above and more? Write 'em down!

b) What types of experiences would you like to have in your ideal life that maybe you don't have now? Do you dine in 5-star restaurants, stay in stellar hotels or get in-home massages every week?

c) List 10 countries, cities, or attractions you'd love to visit.

d) What wildly fun adventures do you attract in your dream life?

e) How big of a role does adventure play in your dream life?

f) Do you travel? If so, where?

g) What types of outside-the-box activities do you engage in (that you likely don't engage in now—or maybe you do!)?

Business & Career

a) In your ideal life, do you own your own business or have a job?

b) No matter what your answer, try answering this: If you could do anything in the world and get paid (generously) for it, what would that be? Don't hold back!

c) What does doing your job or running your business look like on a day-to-day basis? What types of activities do you do? What do you outsource—or not do?

d) How much free time do you have vs. how much time you work? What does your ideal work schedule look like?

e) Who else is involved in your dream business career (i.e. clients, colleagues, team members or contractors, your partner)?

f) Who do you interact with in your dream business or career? How often? And what are your relationships like with these people?

g) What have you achieved (or will you achieve) in your dream life in the career/business department?

h) How do you bring in money in your business or career? What are your actual tasks, or products, services or offers?

i) Where do you work in your dream life—is it at home? In a beautiful office overlooking the city skyline?

Finances

a) How much money would you love to make every year? How about every week? How about every day?

b) What do your investments look like? Where is your money and what is it doing for you?

c) How much debt do you have? What does your relationship to debt look or feel like?

d) How much money do you ideally have in savings? Why that number? How does having that amount in savings make you feel?

e) What does your money allow you to do in your dream life, that you're not able to do now?

f) HOW do you make money? Do you have multiple streams of income, or just one?

g) How much money ideally comes from each of those streams? Or what percentage?

If you answered all of these insightful questions/prompts Congratulations! You've made it. The goal is for you to hopefully feel a lot more clear about what you want (and don't want!) in your dream life.

If you've never done this exercise before, it should have opened your eyes to possibilities and ideas you've possibly never even dared to put on paper. And if you have done it before, I hope it renewed your sense of desire and provided a much-needed dose of clarity around what you want now (not 1 year or 5 years or 10 years ago).

Our dream lives can change over time (just like our desires), so feel free to revisit these questions anytime you need to rediscover or rework your vision for your one wild, precious life.

Now to the FUN part;
The Affirmations

To conquer frustration, one must remain intensely focused on the outcome, NOT the obstacles.

——————————————————— T. F. Hodge

Ready? Let's start with...this Powerful Declaration.

1. My Power Affirmations work whether I believe in them or not.

2. I create new Power Affirmations for myself every day.

3. I repeat my Power Affirmations everyday with emotional intensity, certainty, and faith.

4. My Power Affirmations allow me to consistently tap into the unlimited power of my subconscious mind.

5. My Power Affirmations are now creating thought habits that will guide me to my desired objectives easily and effortlessly.

6. The more I repeat my Power Affirmations with a feeling of certainty, the more accessible these power beliefs are to me when I need them.

7. I feed my subconscious mind thoughts of faith by repeating my power affirmations everyday with physical energy and emotion.

8. My thoughts are creative. My Power Affirmations are now creating the reality I desire.

9. My Power Affirmations positively influence my subconscious mind while I sleep.

10. My imagination now creates whatever I believe and conceive.

11. I now have all the resources I need to achieve my goals easily and effortlessly.

12. Every day in every way I'm getting better and better.

13. I set definite goals and create new Power Affirmations™ to achieve them quickly and easily.

14. Today I am using 100% of my mind's capacity.

15. I now have easy access to the information in my subconscious mind.

16. All subconscious information is being revealed to me now.

17. What I imagine I can do I can do.

18. I receive wisdom and knowledge from God every moment of my life.

19. I am now making amazing progress towards all of my goals.

20. My subconscious mind is now revealing everything I need to know to create and fulfill my mission and purpose in life.

21. I am consciously aware of my beliefs. I only hold onto beliefs that support me.

22. I now see and feel my goals as already accomplished.

23. Using my Power Affirmations, I expand the powers of my subconscious mind every day.

24. Whatever I conceive and believe I can achieve.

25. I create my own luck every day.

26. I now achieve my goals with joy and laughter.

27. I visualize what I want to be and act as if I am already what I visualize.

28. Through consistently repeating my Power Affirmations, I can now create any reality that I desire.

29. My Power Affirmations are now creating habitual thought patterns of success, positive thinking, and positive living.

30. My Power Affirmations are now giving me massive momentum towards the specific results I desire.

31. I am guided and excited. All I need is within me now.

Affirmations To Improve Your Mindset

To conquer frustration, one must remain intensely focused on the outcome, NOT the obstacles.

————————————————— T. F. Hodge

1. I create a safe and secure space for myself wherever I am.

2. I give myself permission to do what is right for me.

3. I am confident in my ability to [fill in the blank].

4. I use my time and talents to help others [fill in the blank].

5. What I love about myself is my ability to [fill in the blank].

6. I feel proud of myself when I [fill in the blank].

7. I give myself space to grow and learn.

8. I allow myself to be who I am without judgment.

9. I listen to my intuition and trust my inner guide.

10. I accept my emotions and let them serve their purpose.

11. I give myself the care and attention that I deserve.

12. My drive and ambition allow me to achieve my goals.

13. I share my talents with the world by [fill in the blank].

14. I am good at helping others to [fill in the blank].

15. I am always headed in the right direction.

16. I trust that I am on the right path.

17. I am creatively inspired by the world around me.

18. My mind is full of brilliant ideas.

19. I put my energy into things that matter to me.

20. I trust myself to make the right decision.

21. I am becoming closer to my true self every day.

22. I am grateful to have people in my life who [fill in the blank].

23. I am learning valuable lessons from myself every day.

24. I am at peace with who I am as a person.

25. I make a difference in the world by simply existing in it.

26. I am a strong and capable person.

27. I can get through anything in my life.

28. Hard times do not get the best of me.

29. I have the ability to overcome any obstacle

30. I am a strong person.

31. I can solve any problem.

32. I will not let fear take control of me.

33. I can and will survive anything life throws at me.

34. I have the strength and courage to get through any situation.

35. I welcome challenges into my life.

36. I am ready to become the best version of myself.

37. I am enjoying being the best version of myself.

Dr. Stem
Be Encouraged

EAGLES DON'T TAKE FLIGHT LESSONS FROM CHICKENS.

Affirmations For Gratitude

I don't regret the things that I have done. I just regret the things I didn't do.

Lucas

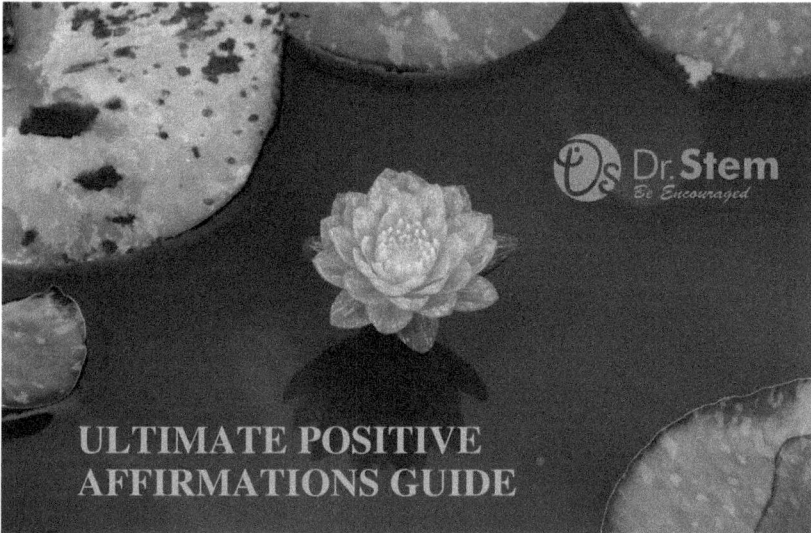

ULTIMATE POSITIVE
AFFIRMATIONS GUIDE

1. I am thankful for my safe and secure home.

2. I gratefully receive the lessons that each experience brings.

3. I am grateful for the constant flow of money through my life.

4. I realize how fortunate I am that so many people love me.

5. I have access to nourishing food and clean water, and I am so thankful.

6. I appreciate all of the people involved in bringing food to my table.

7. Every person I meet can teach me something. I am grateful for their wisdom.

8. I realize the gift of this precious human life.

9. I love and appreciate my beautiful family.

10. My friends enrich my life beyond measure; I am so thankful for each and every one.

11. My pets are a source of comfort and unconditional love. I am so lucky to have them.

12. I revere nature in all her glory, and I love connecting with her every day.

13. I appreciate all the things my wonderful body allows me to do.

14. My kids help me develop patience, kindness, and playfulness. I'm so grateful for them.

15. I am thankful for my mistakes because they have made me stronger.

16. I give thanks for each exquisite moment.

17. I see and appreciate the light in everyone, including myself.

18. I am grateful to the universe for manifesting all the wonderful things in my life so far.

19. I recognize every blessing, no matter how small.

20. I am thankful for the ability to learn, develop, and grow.

21. I see abundance all around me, and I feel so blessed.

22. Thankfully, I have the power to make my dreams come true.

23. I am so grateful for all the love in my life – given and received.

24. I recognize the opportunities the universe presents, and I give thanks for each one.

25. With a sense of gratitude, I see the world in a new light. Each day is an opportunity and a gift.

26. I am thankful to my parents for loving me and teaching me. I know they did their very best.

27. I appreciate my strength and resilience. I know I can survive and thrive.

28. To every teacher who has helped my learning and shaped me into the person I am today, I will be eternally grateful.

29. I am thankful for my unique creativity and my capacity to enrich other people's lives.

30. I am grateful for my sense of gratitude – I know it is the way to joy, peace, and the life of my dreams.

31. I am eternally grateful for the love I am capable of giving, and for the love I have yet to receive.

32. Whatever has happened, and whatever does happen, I'm certain that I can be grateful again.

33. I am grateful for the helpful guides that sometimes appear in disguise to usher me back to love.

34. I am grateful now, and that is keeping the door open for more blessings.

35. Even devastation is an opportunity for transformation, and my gratitude evolves as I do.

36. "There is a calmness to a life lived in gratitude, a quiet joy." – Ralph H. Blum

37. I welcome all of the ways the universe wants to bless me.

38. If I approach this situation/experience/person with appreciation, I will be held in the arms of abundance.

39. Whatever I see, I trust that the universe is supporting my highest good. I choose to see this season of my life, then, through the eyes of appreciation, as best as I can.

40. My thanksgiving is perpetual; it survives every obstacle because I am willing to keep it alive.

41. The feeling of gratefulness expands my perspective and opens me up to new ways of living happily in this world; it's as if the whole universe is in my heart.

42. I'm willing to see beauty where others see nothing; I can look beyond a rock and uncover the diamond. For the rocks and the diamonds, I am thankful, because life is a rich experience that includes everything.

43. The more you pay attention to what's already working in your life, the better it gets.

44. My thanksgiving extends far beyond my thoughts; I bring a grateful spirit to each step and action I take.

45. I choose to be thankful for the light of this new morning, and for renewed energy and strength to be who I know I can be.

46. I shine the light of appreciation on an otherwise dark situation; there is no darkness that can escape that light for long.

47. I accept my burdens and I accept my blessings, and so I transform my burdens into my blessings.

48. I partner with peace today, and I do this through the power of keeping a grateful heart.

49. I fully accept the joy that wants to surface in my life, and I accept it now in gratitude.

50. Give thanks for your ability to give anything in life, even if all you can give is a "thank you."

51. I choose to see peace instead. I am willing to trust that my life is exactly as it's meant to be. I can relax a little and be thankful for what I have now.

52. In truth, my gratitude is an absolute magnet for the manifestation of all that I want.

Affirmations For:
A Powerful Self-Image
& Self-Love

Failure is the opportunity to begin again, this time more intelligently than before.

— Henry Ford

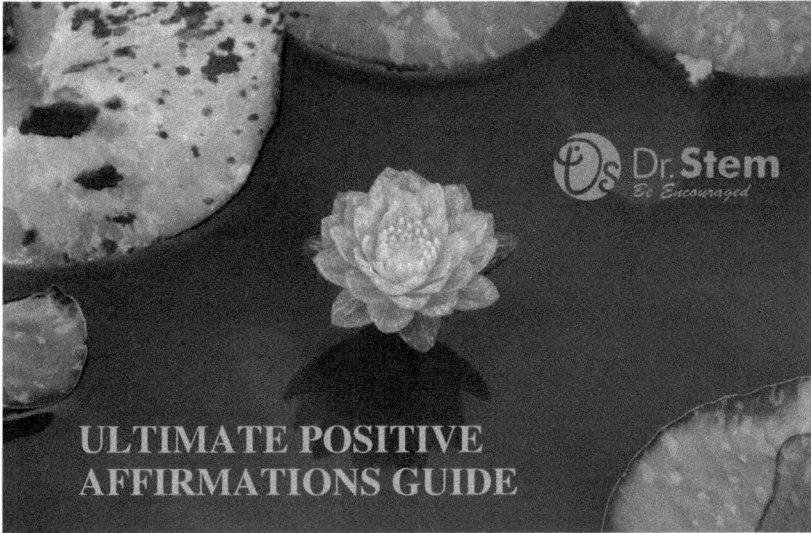

ULTIMATE POSITIVE AFFIRMATIONS GUIDE

1. I am now filled with faith, certainty, and confidence. I now feel these emotions in my body.

2. I am now confident and assertive.

3. I now walk and move with assurance, poise, and personal power.

4. I am now a powerful and charismatic personality.

5. I am growing more and more attractive every day.

6. My confidence and competence are exploding massively every day.

7. I am now friendly, outgoing, and confident.

8. I am now bold and courageous. I now seize my opportunities immediately.

9. I now have the ability to change anything in my life that I choose to change. I take complete responsibility for my life.

10. When I speak to others, I look them straight in the eye and speak with confidence knowing that I am equal to every person I meet regardless of their social status or accomplishments.

11. I can now create a state of total certainty and confidence at a moment's notice anytime I need it.

12. I now move my body with poise and confidence.

13. Every time I close my eyes and breathe deeply, my confidence expands and fills my whole being.

14. I now see myself as exactly the person I want to be confident, self- assured, healthy, and prosperous.

15. I now hold myself and other people in high esteem.

16. Every day in every way I am growing more and more confident.

17. My confident energy, enthusiasm, and passion are increasing massively every day.

18. Because I am committed to constant and never-ending improvement, my performance is improving every day.

19. What I imagine I can do, I can do.

20. I am now fearless, courageous, and bold.

21. I receive wisdom and knowledge from my subconscious mind every moment of my life.

22. I apply my faith with consistent acts of courage.

23. The expression on my face now communicates certainty and confidence.

24. I am now a highly charismatic and powerful person.

25. I now inspire and expand my imagination with enthusiasm.

26. I now relive the most joyous moments of my life. And these moments inspire me to greater confidence and a greater feeling of self-worth.

27. I immerse myself in a powerful environment on a regular basis.

28. I act as if I already have all the confidence, I need and desire.

29. I speak to myself and others with confidence, certainty, and conviction.

30. I now take complete and total control of my internal images, dialog, and feelings.

31. My subconscious mind now communicates confidence, certainty, and power to the subconscious minds of others.

32. My thoughts, presence, charm, and charisma now inspire others to greater self-confidence and personal power.

33. I now radiate confidence and certainty in the presence of other people.

34. When I speak, the tone of my voice communicates strength, courage, and confidence.

35. I am now confident, assertive, and decisive in every situation.

36. I now create outstanding confidence by repeatedly rehearsing in my mind and imagining the results I want in advance.

37. I am now an outstanding leader who leads with confidence.

38. I increase my self-confidence by increasing my skills and abilities everyday.

39. As I rehearse the results I want in my thoughts before they happen, my skill and confidence expand massively.

40. Other people find me to be a fascinating and interesting person.

41. I consciously choose the emotional state that I am in at all times.

42. I am now raising my standards in all the major areas of my life and am holding myself to those standards at all times.

43. I now control the pictures, sounds, and feelings that I create in my mind.

44. I am now comfortable with a high level of uncertainty in my life knowing that without great risks there are no great rewards.

45. I now face challenging situations of great uncertainty with a feeling of absolute certainty and confidence that I can transform any challenge or set back to my advantage.

46. I am now positively adventurous and outrageous.

47. I now put myself into new positively challenging situations everyday.

I now set new and higher standards for myself and I step up to every challenge in a state of absolute certainty and unstoppable confidence

Affirmations For:
Pursuing & Achieving
Your Dreams & Goals

Too many of us are not living in our dreams because we are living our fears.

Les Brown

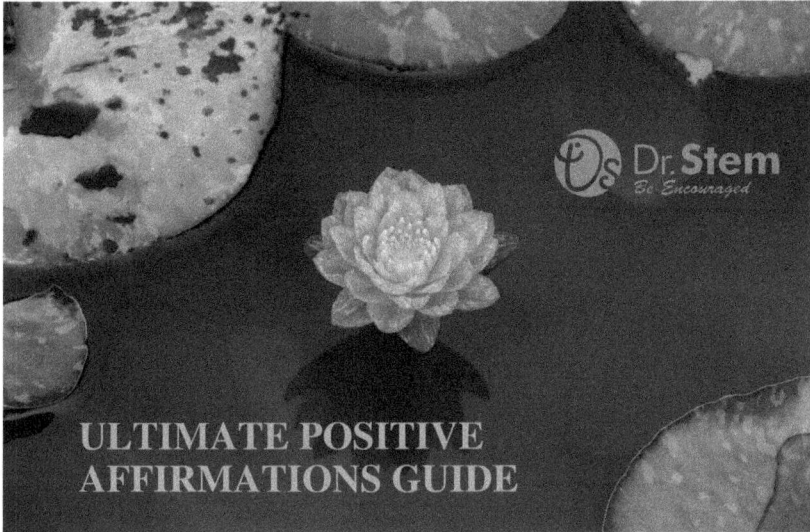

ULTIMATE POSITIVE
AFFIRMATIONS GUIDE

1. I now put my body into a peak state of absolute certainty knowing that I can create any positive result that I am committed to.

2. I am now living a life of design rather than a life of reaction.

3. I am now absolutely clear about the specific results I want in every area of my life.

4. I now step up with total power and passion to take whatever positive action is necessary to achieve my desired results.

5. I now make my future my present. My future is now.

6. I now celebrate the achievement of my goals before they occur in the physical world.

7. I now celebrate my achievements in advance.

8. Whenever I set a definite goal, I take immediate action towards its attainment to create and sustain massive momentum.

9. I am now spending my time, energy, and emotion on the goals that are most important to me rather than responding to the demands of other people. I am in control.

10. Urgency is not my friend. Through results-focused planning and delegating to others, I minimize the amount of time I spend addressing the urgent demands of other people.

11. I now do only what I do best and get other people to do the rest.

12. I now delegate tasks that do not require my direct attention and focus to other people.

13. My subconscious mind now provides me with the specific massive action plans I need to attain my desired results.

14. My subconscious mind is now consistently presenting me with updated plans to achieve my goals even when I am playing, eating, or sleeping.

16. I am now highly flexible. I carefully monitor the results that I am getting and quickly adjust my actions until I receive the specific results I desire.

17. I accelerate my progress towards my desired results by studying other people who have been outstanding in that area.

17. I increase my hunger and desire to achieve my goals every day.

18. I now carefully measure and manage my progress towards my desired results every day.

19. Using tapes, books, music, and anything else around me that is easily accessible, I now create a controlled environment that keeps my mind focused on my primary outcomes every day.

20. I do not adapt to my environment. I persist in making my environment adapt to me.

21. All of my internal images, dialog and feelings are now pulling me towards the results I desire. I am totally committed and congruent.

22. I am now focused on the results I want, driven by a passionate purpose, and charted with massive action plans.

23. I now see things exactly the way they are, exactly the way I want them, and now take massive action to close that gap.

24. I now prepare a results-oriented daily plan every evening for the following day.

25. I feed my momentum monster everyday by consistently taking results-focused action.

26. When I reach a definite decision, I commit and resolve to the achievement of the end result I desire.

27. I now create magic moments for myself, my family, and friends.

Affirmations For:
Self-Conficence

You know you are on the road to success if you would do your job, and not be paid for it.

— Oprah Winfrey

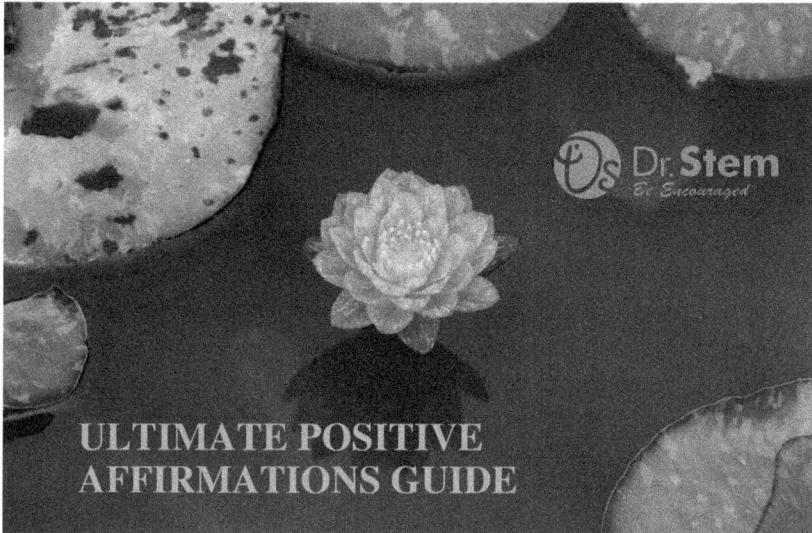

ULTIMATE POSITIVE AFFIRMATIONS GUIDE

1. I am aware of my gift to the world and share it freely

2. I am compassionate with others and myself

3. I am a positive being, aware of my potential

4. There are no blocks I cannot overcome

5. I love to meet other people and make new friends.

6. I am my best source of motivation.

7. Challenges are opportunities to grow and improve.

8. I attract positive people into my life.

9. I make a difference by showing up every day and doing my best.

10. I am becoming a better version of myself one day at a time.

11. I am worthy of having what I want.

12. I am grateful for my journey and its lessons.

13. I accept compliments easily.

14. Everything is possible.

15. I am creative and open to new solutions.

16. I choose to embrace the mystery of life.

17. I already have what I need.

18. What I want is already here or on its way.

19. I appreciate all that I have.

20. I allow everything to be as it is.

21. I enjoy going with the flow.

22. The more I let go, the better I feel.

23. I live from a place of abundance.

24. I release anything that doesn't serve me.

25. I believe in my abilities and express my true self with ease.

26. All I need is within me.

27. I am stronger than I seem.

28. I am braver than I think.

29. I have unshakable faith.

30. Miracles are taking place in my life.

31. I have the power to do the most incredible things

32. I'm confident in myself and my abilities

33. I always make the best decision for myself

34. I am in charge of my life

35. My confidence in myself grows more and more every day

36. My confidence is constantly increasing

37. I'm a magnet for success

38. I can achieve anything I put my mind to

39. I love myself

40. I believe in myself and my abilities

41. I have the power to accomplish everything I need to do today

42. I know I'm making a difference

43. My clients love to work with me

44. I'm constantly inspiring people around me

45. I'm proud of myself and my achievements

46. I wake up each morning feeling confident and empowered

47. Confidence is my birth right

48. I'm successful in everything I do

49. I attract success by being my authentic self

50. Every day in every way I'm becoming more confident

51. All my thoughts, plans and ideas lead me straight to success

52. I'm radiant with confidence, certainty, and optimism

53. I exude confidence

54. I'm confident in the decisions I make

55. I trust myself and my intuition

56. Every decision I make leads me towards my desires

57. Confidence is my middle name

58. I live each day feeling confident and grateful

59. I love seeing my confidence grow every single day

60. I radiate confidence and positivity

61. I am confident

always wonder why birds choose to stay in the same place when they can fly anywhere on Earth...

Dr. Stem
Be Encouraged

...then I ask myself the same question.

Affirmations For:
Self-Esteem

*Even the greatest were beginners at some point.
Don't be afraid to take that **first step.***

Les Brown

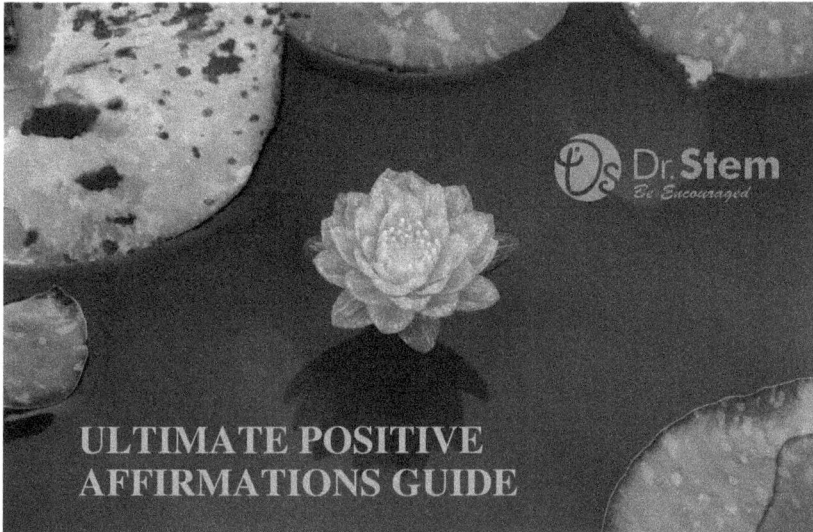

ULTIMATE POSITIVE AFFIRMATIONS GUIDE

1. I am a special person. There's nobody else like me.

2. I love myself.

3. I love myself more and more each day.

4. I am worthy of love.

5. I am worthy of happiness.

6. I am worthy of success.

7. I deserve to be paid well for my skills.

8. I am supported in all I do in life.

9. I have the power to create the life I want.

10. I am beautiful, intelligent, fun, and full of life.

11. I am a successful and happy person.

12. People value my work, my time, and my love.

Affirmations For:
Good Health

With slight efforts, how can we obtain great results. it is foolish to even desire it.

Euripides

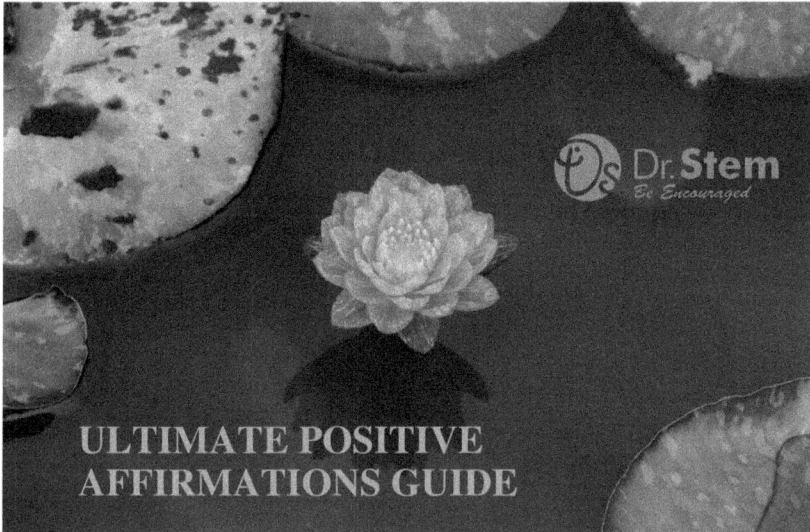

ULTIMATE POSITIVE
AFFIRMATIONS GUIDE

1. My health, energy, and vitality are increasing every day.

2. I am a lean, mean, fat burning, muscle building machine.

3. I am growing more and more attractive every day.

4. Divine life now flows through every cell in my body.

5. I now eat all the right foods for optimum health, energy, and peak performance.

6. My body is healing and regenerating itself every day.

7. With every deep breath I take, my body is burning fat and creating massive energy, health, and vitality.

8. My body burns fat regardless of what I eat.

9. I now see myself filled with health, energy, and enthusiasm.

10. I now have all the energy I need.

11. I create good health habits quickly and easily.

12. My body now eliminates all toxins quickly, easily, and healthfully.

13. I am now relaxed and filled with peace of mind. In my relaxed state, my body repairs and heals itself quickly.

14. All of the cells in my body exist in harmony and peace with every other cell in my body.

15. I get a full night's rest every day.

16. When I sleep, my mind is at peace and the healing powers within my body are magnified.

17. The creative intelligence which made my body is now transforming every cell according to nature's perfect pattern.

18. My healing thoughts are now going deep into my subconscious mind and bringing total and continuous healing to my body.

19. I now enjoy a large variety of water rich foods that fully cleanse and nourish every cell in my body.

20. I drink an abundance of pure water every day.

21. I sleep in peace and I wake in joy. Through peaceful sleep, my body and mind are renewed and restored to perfect health.

Dr. Stem
Be Encouraged

Affirmations For:
Pursuing Happiness

When you know what you want, and want it badly enough, you will find a way to get it.

Jim Rohn

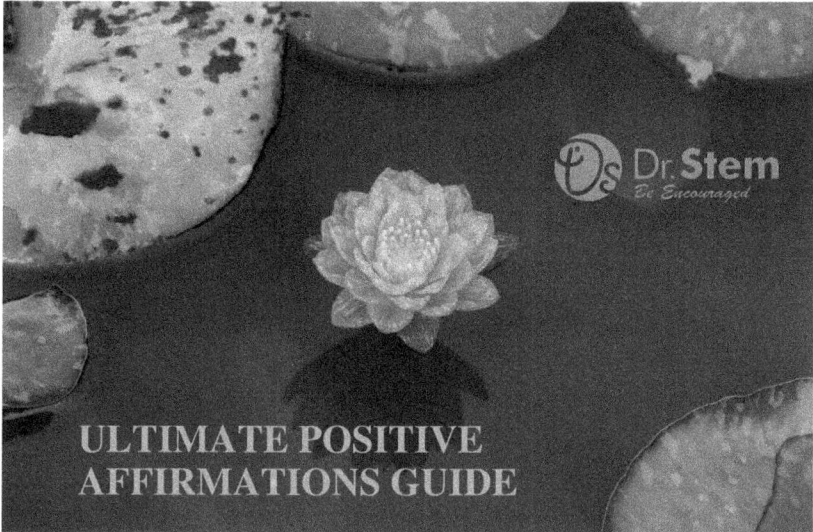

ULTIMATE POSITIVE
AFFIRMATIONS GUIDE

1. I deserve to be happy, healthy, wealthy, and successful

2. I am allowing myself to be consistent and genuinely happy

3. An angel like me doesn't deserve all this sadness

4. I am worthy of feeling happy all day, everyday

5. It is possible for me to feel happy all day, every day.

6. I am allowing myself to feel happy all day, everyday

7. It is easy for me to feel happy all day, everyday

8. It is natural for me to feel happy every day, all day.

9. I am attracting and allowing money to come to me in ways that will make me really, really happy and wealthy

10. I am unique and I feel great about being alive and being me

11. Amazing opportunities exist for me in every aspect of my life

12. I fall in love over and over again

13. I love being loved and loving this best lover of my life

14. I deserve all of the good things that are in my life

15. I'm able to be happy for people that aren't in my life anymore when I see them doing well.

16. I choose to create a happy peaceful life

17. I attract a loving happy family for myself

18. I deserve to be happy, healthy, wealthy, and successful

19. I'm good with who I am, I 'm proud of who I'm becoming

20. I'm committing myself to live a happy life

21. I don't need to show off to prove that I'm doing well

22. I'm creating the life I deserve to live

23. I don't need to live in a way that will impress others. I need to live my life in a way that will keep me happy.

24. I'm going to accomplish all of my dreams. I'm going to think and work them into existence.

25. I am happy

26. I am accomplishing all of my dreams and goals in divine order under grace.

27. I'm not selfish if I focus on myself for a little bit. I need to make sure I'm

28. Okay and happy.

29. I will choose the happiness of this moment, instead of the pain of the past.

30. I am a radiant and joyous person.

31. People hating on me will not stop my happiness. My success is the best answer.

32. I am good at loving others and I make others happy.

33. The only person I want to be is a better version of myself

34. I'm going to reach every goal I set for myself.

35. I'm reaching every goal I set for myself. I'm not giving up on any my dreams.

36. Happiness and love flow freely from me

37. Every day in every way I am getting happier and happier

38. I am surrounded by loving people, cuddly creatures, and happy moments.

39. I am open to laughter today

40. When I can control how I feel, I can control my future

41. I'm making the conscious, continued effort to heal and be happy. It's great.

42. I now choose to be as happy as possible in positive and healthy ways.

43. I abandon my old habits and take up new, more positive ones.

44. I am worthy of being loved, being happy and doing what brings me joy.

45. I choose to be positive.

46. I choose only to see the positive

47. I choose to think only the positive

48. I choose what experiences to have

49. I choose how to respond to circumstance

50. I choose to feel good

51. I choose to be grateful

52. I choose to be happy

53. I want to be happy rather than looking happy

54. I give myself permission to be happy

55. I'm proud of myself because the work I did today got me a little bit closer to living my dreams.

Affirmations For:
Women

— Henry S. Haskins

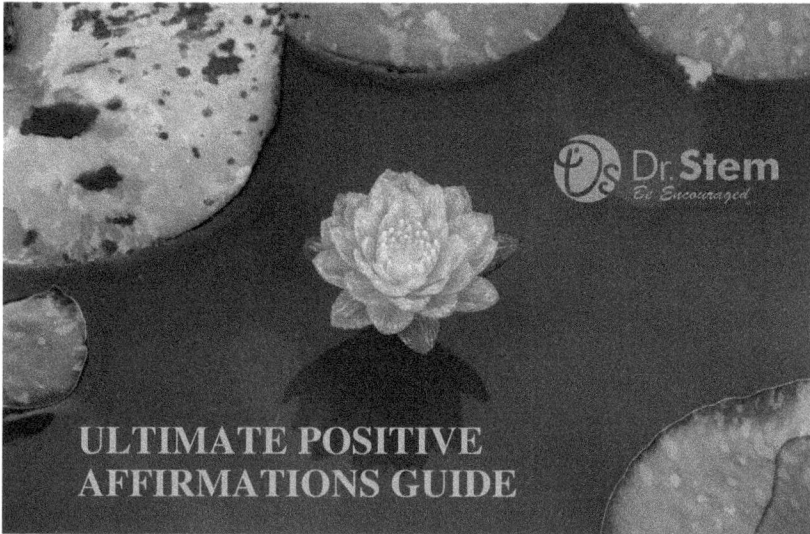

ULTIMATE POSITIVE AFFIRMATIONS GUIDE

1. I am at peace with my body and accept it as it is. It was created to do amazing things.

2. I love living in my unique female body. It has features that are distinctive and make me who I am.

3. I am attractive just as I am. I don't need to change anything. I'm not perfect, but I am still beautiful.

4. I love my body and I take care of it through healthy eating and exercise. I respect my body and am thankful for all it can do.

5. I am responsible for what happens to my body, so I treat it with love, respect, and care.

6. I exercise my body daily with ease and am amazed at the ways it can bend, move, stretch, and pose.

7. I am a strong, confident women and will only continue to become stronger.

8. I am patient with my body when it needs rest, healing, and recovery.

9. I respect my body's needs and treat it with the kindness that it deserves.

10. I choose to release love, happiness, and gratitude into the world today. Life is precious and beautiful, and I choose to focus on the positive.

11. I am grateful for this wonderful day and the endless possibilities it has to offer. I know something great is in store for me.

12. No matter what goes on today, I know the truth that I am a radiant, powerful, and free woman.

13. I embrace my best self today. I live in a way that brings tranquility, joy, and pleasure to myself and others.

14. I know I am alive for a reason. Today, I honor my purpose and inspire people around me to do the same.

15. I don't need anyone else or anything to complete me because I am already complete just as I am.

16. Instead of judging other people, I only judge myself on whether or not I am being the best person I can be. This is a better use of my time.

17. I maintain a positive attitude today despite any hurdles that come my way. I have what it takes to succeed.

18. I push fear aside to take action in spite of perceived limitation because I know all of my needs are being met by the universe.

19. I embrace this day as a chance to be better than I was yesterday. I make only the best decisions for my life today.

20. I am exactly where I need to be. I welcome the challenges and opportunities that I am facing today, and I choose to learn and grow.

21. I only plant positive seeds in the world today. I do not waste one precious moment in anger, hatred, or envy.

22. I am on earth for a reason, and I am committed to living a positive life and being a positive influence on others.

23. I take responsibility for my own happiness today. I don't allow anyone else to have the power over my mood because I am in control.

24. I look and feel radiant knowing I have so much to offer the world.

25. I love myself and like myself. I choose to focus on my positive qualities and how I can use them to improve myself and the world.

Affirmations For Men

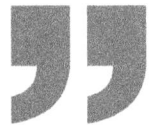

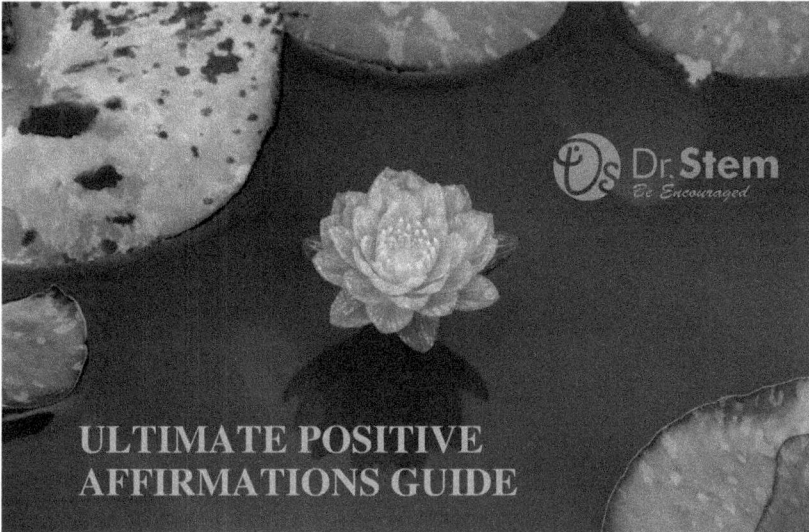

ULTIMATE POSITIVE
AFFIRMATIONS GUIDE

1. I am loving and complete

2. It is ok for me to be free of emotional, personal, and physical holds

3. I don't always have to be in charge

4. I can allow myself to relax and let go

5. It's ok for me to cry and release my emotions

6. I am focused and never quit

7. I am committed to maximizing my success

8. A challenge brings out the best in me

9. If I am to fail, I will fail forward

10. My dreams are there to achieve

11. My confidence has no limit

12. I will do what it takes to achieve my goals

13. I will seize every opportunity presented to me

14. I am prepared to go the extra mile

15. Hard work fulfills me

16. Success comes naturally to me

17. Success is my driving force

18. I love what I do

19. I believe in myself

20. I'm worthy of success

21. I choose what I become

22. I deserve success

23. I excel in all that I do

24. I set high standards for myself

25. I am focused

26. I am patient

27. I trust the universe

28. I respect myself

29. I will be great

30. I have limitless potential

31. I have an opportunity

32. I will do whatever it takes

33. Nothing can stop me

34. I will achieve my goals

35. I see my goal clearly

36. I am determined

37. I see challenges as opportunities for growth

38. I am the architect of my life

39. I'm a magnet for success

40. I'm right where I need to be

41. I live my life without fear

42. I feel things falling into place

43. I like myself

44. Success is second nature to me

45. Mistakes are a steppingstone to success

46. I am proud of my success

47. I think only of success

48. All problems have a solution

49. I am in charge of my life

50. My power comes from within me

51. I find inspiration easily

52. Consistency is key to my success

53. Everything I touch is a success

54. I am persistent

55. Life is full of choices. I choose success

Dr. Stem
Be Encouraged

Affirmations For Men & Women's Personal and Professional Growth

It's easy to attack and destroy an act of creation.
It's a lot more difficult to perform one.

———————————————— Chuck Palahniuk

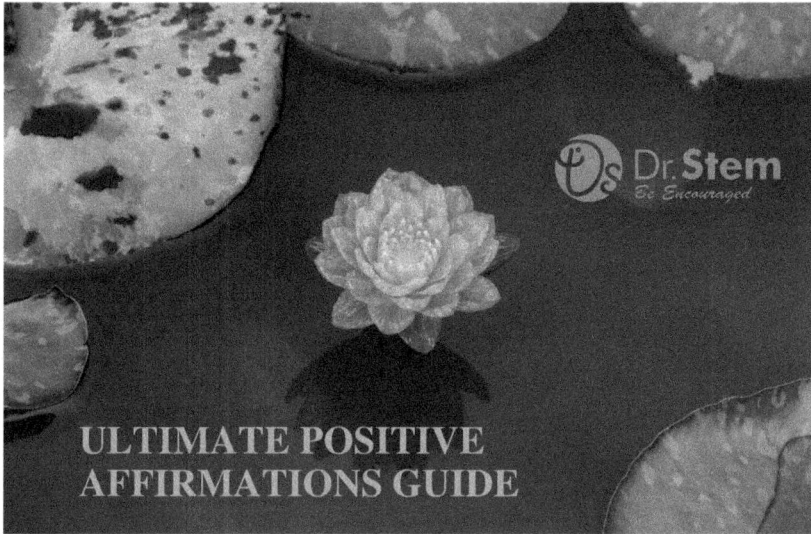

**ULTIMATE POSITIVE
AFFIRMATIONS GUIDE**

1. I am overflowing with renewed confidence every day. I continue to grow and become a stronger woman for myself and for the people around me.

2. I reach any goal I set my mind to. If I dream it, I can do it. No goal is out of reach.

3. I never stop learning and see opportunities for growth everywhere. I improve every day for the rest of my life.

4. I am better than I was at this point last year, and I am becoming better and better with each passing day.

5. I am patient with myself and accept that positive change takes time.

6. My best self is emerging every day.

7. There is nothing stopping me from growing.

8. I ask for what I want because I deserve it. I honor my desires today and always.

9. Regardless of any situation that confronts me, I am blessed. I am blessed with every lesson I learn from hardships I face. I continue to grow in light of all of the positive and negative things that come my way.

10. I reach my goals even if I make mistakes because I know there is nothing to stop me from getting what I want.

11. Rather than being discouraged by how far I have left to go, I am grateful for how far I have already come.

12. I do not allow other people to hold me back from achieving my goals. I give myself permission to walk my own path and allow other people to do the same.

13. I forgive myself and other people to release myself from any past pain. When I forgive, I am free. I am leaving the past in the past, and I am only living for the present and the future.

14. I know what I want, and I know I deserve it. I take responsibility for everything I have brought into my life.

15. I release my attachment to anything that does not serve me. I don't let anything, or anybody hold me back. I am finished with negativity in my life.

16. I seize opportunities and make things happen.

17. My past does not define who I am today.

18. I accept that I cannot change the past. I focus on my future and move forward in my life.

19. I do one thing every day to make consistent progress toward my dreams. I surpass other people's expectations because I am exceptional.

20. I choose to learn from the positive and negative events of the past so that I continue to make progress towards my bright future.

21. I do not need to control everything around me.

22. I focus on allowing the best things to happen.

23. I know that whatever is supposed to will be.

24. I am living my own version of happiness that has nothing to do with anyone else. I am happy for anyone else who is happy and other people are happy for me.

25. Even if I do something wrong, I go back and find another way. I create a new course of action. I do not stop.

26. I am ready to commit to my ideal life, and the world works along with me.

27. I take the first step and the rest comes naturally.

28. Rather than complaining about not having enough time today, I use the time I have in a way that is in line with my values and goals.

29. I make a conscious effort to make the best of every moment I am given today.

30. I trust my own wisdom and intuition. I am the only person who knows what is best for me.

31. I am open to any new opportunity that comes my way. I do not believe that my options are limited.

32. I am ready to create more success in my life and am ready to release any excuses. I am productive and focused on attaining results.

33. I am free to create my ideal reality for the future. I have a choice in every situation that I face. There is nothing that can get between me and my best self.

34. I love my face and all my features and see my imperfections as signs of a life well-lived.

35. I am a source of knowledge that people seek out when they need information.

36. I am constantly amazed by my body and its abilities.

37. I exude confidence when I go out in the world and others see it in me.

38. I hold my head up high and put a smile on my face every day.

39. I let go of my need to impress other people. There is nothing that I need to prove. I accept myself just as I am.

40. I am excited to show the world who I am and everything I have to offer. No one can stop me from meeting my goals.

41. I am brave and willing to embrace my full power. I have complete control over my actions and my life.

42. I am the president of my life and no one else can take that role. I trust myself to make the best decisions for my life.

43. I have infinite possibilities today. I love life and I am ready to take inspired and motivated action on my goals.

44. I don't have to wait until I feel ready to act on my goals. The timing will never be right. I'm ready now.

45. I will take action despite any fear of failure. No matter what, I am proud of myself for trying.

46. I am not afraid of the unknown because I know I can overcome all the challenges that come my way.

47. I embrace my full potential, even if it makes other people uncomfortable. I do not play small. I am supposed to do big things.

48. I radiate respect and love and I get it in return.

49. I am cultured and smart, yet able to stay humble.

50. Because of my high self-esteem, I easily accept compliments and give them in return.

51. I deserve everything that is good. I do not have any need for misery and suffering.

52. I accept my past mistakes and let them go. They don't

define me. I move forward with confidence in my essential goodness and good judgment with ease.

53. My mind is full of caring, healthy, positive, and loving thoughts which transform into my life experiences.

54. I act with confidence and have a plan, and I accept that plans are open to change.

55. I love challenges because they bring out the best in me.

56. I am a powerful creator, and I create the life that I want starting today.

57. I am kind, loving, and compassionate. I truly care for other people.

58. It comes naturally to be confident in myself. I don't need to question my confidence.

59. I don't need to be perfect. I am already good enough and I am worthy of a great life already.

60. I do not have a need to compare myself to other people. I only judge myself by my own standards of success. I am enough just the way I am.

61. I channel love, positivity, and energy to all the people around me.

62. Positive Affirmations for Women While at Work

63. I practice self-care and recognise when I need to take a break. I feel good about taking care of myself.

64. I am successful and confident in my abilities to do my job.

65. I am a competent member of the team. I have the knowledge and skills that I need right now.

66. I move at the perfect pace. I do not need to speed up or slow down.

67. I embrace success. The words "I can't" are not something I say. I refuse to believe even my own excuses. I am unstoppable.

68. I take my goals seriously. I am aware that my time on earth is finite. I respect my life by doing the things I love.

69. I refuse to overcommit myself. I am able to say "no" when I need to. I protect my time because I deserve it and it is invaluable.

70. My work is a self-transformative process that brings me inner peace, proper health, and prosperity.

71. I'm almost at the finish line. I know I have what it takes to meet my goals.

72. My hard work, humility, and persistence will pay off. None of my work is going to waste.

73. The passion I have for my work allows me to create true value. I am lucky to have a job that provides me with the finances I need to live a good life.

74. I work extremely hard and always do my personal best.

I believe in myself and I know I can do anything. I deserve all of the positive things that come my way in life.

75. The work that I do benefits the society in which I live, and I am a valuable part of my community.

76. I do not give up when things get difficult. I keep working until I finish what I started.

77. My work is fulfilling, inspiring, and enriching. I am not only helping myself, but I am also helping others.

78. I see myself reaching the pinnacle of success as I envision it and work hard every day until I am where I want to be in my career.

79. I bring something unique to the table that no one else can and that makes me uniquely valuable to my company.

80. I am a capable leader. Others are attracted to my charisma at work and look up to me during times of crisis.

81. I stay true to my values and my authentic self. I do not compromise for anyone else. My success will come without compromise.

82. I do not need to prove my worth. My work is enough for people to see it's value. Woolf recognize my worth without having to be told.

83. Others recognize my work for its excellence, and I am proud to call it my own.

84. Other people's successes empower me to keep growing. I am happy for anyone who accomplishes their goals and I will strive to continue to accomplish mine.

85. I accept constructive criticism and welcome self-improvement. I offer constructive criticism to help others around me.

86. My voice matters and I am confident to speak up when I want to. People listen to me because my words are valuable.

87. Success is possible for me because I have the right opportunities, and I take advantage of them when I see them. I know the path I need to take in order to succeed.

88. I have more than enough value to offer in my job. I continue to flourish and gain experience and succeed to levels that I never expected.

89. My mind is focused, and I have clarity in all that I do at work. I do not succumb to distractions.

90. I am on my way to greatness. I go the extra mile to meet people whom I admire and respect. I take one step farther than anyone else around me.

91. I am committed to my success and will not back down. I enjoy taking action when I have a goal so I can acquire the lifestyle that I dream of.

92. I am calm when I am faced with conflict. I can brush off negativity easily, and I can agree to disagree. I enjoy being the bigger person and taking the high road.

Biblical Affirmations
For Men & Women

Life is what we make it, always has been, always will be.

———————————————— Grandma Moses

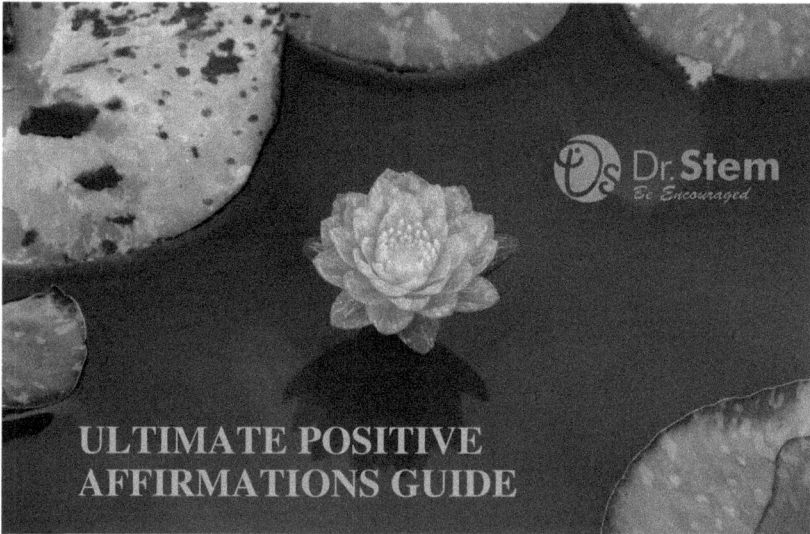

ULTIMATE POSITIVE
AFFIRMATIONS GUIDE

1. Every morning I am renewed and energized by the Lord's abiding love. Lamentations 3:22-23

-   *The steadfast love of the LORD never ceases; his mercies never come to an end; they are new every morning; great is your faithfulness.*

2. I am strong and courageous because I know God is with me in every moment. Deuteronomy 31:6

-   *Be strong and courageous. Do not be afraid or terrified because of them, or the LORD your God goes with you; he will never leave you nor forsake you.*

3. I am so filled with God's love that there is no room for fear or anxiety. John 4:18

-   *There is no fear in love. But perfect love drives out fear because fear has to do with punishment. The one who fears is not made perfect in love.*

4. I am strong and confident and filled with energy because God's love renews me. Isaiah 40:31

- *But they who wait for the LORD shall renew their strength; they shall mount up with wings like eagles; they shall run and not be weary; they shall walk and not faint.*

5. Achieving my goals is easy because I know God is directing me and supporting my every effort. Mark 10:27

- *Jesus looked at them and said, 'With man it is impossible, but not with God. For all things are possible with God.'*

6. With God's help, I always know the best actions to take and the right decisions to make. Proverbs 3:3-6

- *Trust in the LORD with all your heart, and do not lean on your own understanding. In all your ways acknowledge him, and he will make straight your paths.*

7. My faith in the Lord sustains me and gives me the strength to do what I need to do today and every day. Matthews 17:20

- *Our faith can move mountains.*

8. I know that good things are in store for me because God's plan is perfect in every way. Jeremiah 29:11

- *"For I know the plans I have for you," declares the LORD, "plans to prosper you and not to harm you, plans to give you hope and a future."*

9. I am uplifted and blessed beyond measure because the kingdom of heaven is promised to me. Matthew 5:3–5

   - *"Blessed are the poor in spirit, for theirs is the kingdom of heaven. Blessed are those who mourn, for they will be comforted. Blessed are the meek, for they will inherit the earth."*

Daily Affirmations for Creating Loving Relationships

Don't be afraid of change, it is leading you to a new beginning.

Anonymous

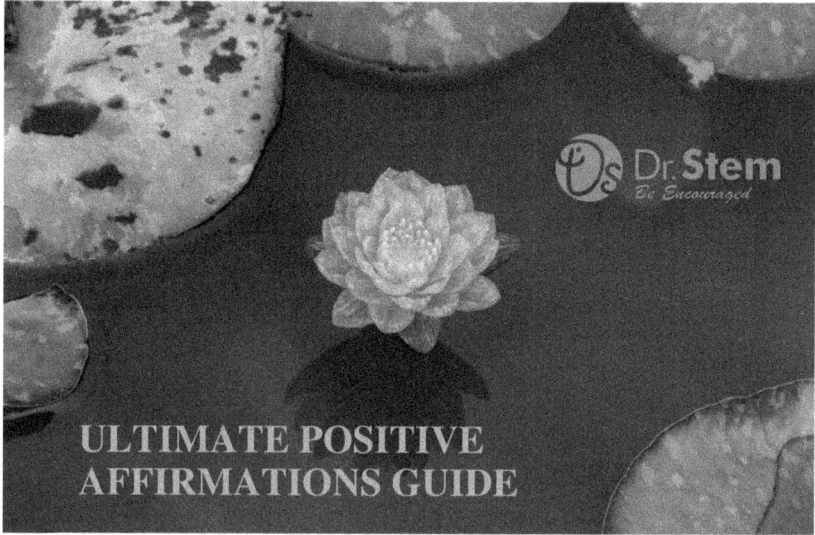

ULTIMATE POSITIVE
AFFIRMATIONS GUIDE

1. I now make good friends quickly and easily.

2. Good people are attracted to me every day. They want to meet me.

3. I now put other people at ease quickly and easily.

4. I now hold myself and other people in high esteem.

5. I now surround myself with positive, proactive people.

6. I always create harmony with others through cooperative effort.

7. I will succeed by attracting to myself the cooperation of other people.

8. I will encourage others to help me because of my willingness to help other people.

9. I will cause other people to believe in me because I believe in them and in myself.

10. I actively listen to what others say without interrupting them.

11. I create synergistic, positive relationships that are fair, honest, and healthy.

12. All my facial expressions are now pleasant and pleasing to myself and other people.

13. When I greet people, I great them with gladness in my being.

14. I now have a magnetic, warm handshake.

15. When people first meet me, they like me instantly.

16. My subconscious mind properly prepares the subconscious mind of every person I meet before I meet them.

17. I now accomplish my goals with the benefits to others in mind.

18. I listen to others carefully before responding.

19. I now develop cooperative alliances with others towards definite, specific objectives quickly and easily.

20. I now have a keen understanding of myself and of other people.

21. I treat every person I meet with respect, mercy, tolerance, and understanding.

22. I now look for the good in every person I meet, and I find it.

23. I inspire and empower others to greatness.

24. I now have favor in the eyes of every person I meet.

25. I now have a highly pleasing personality.

26. All of my contacts with other people are smooth and pleasant.

27. I express my honest and sincere appreciation and praise for others easily and often.

28. I arouse a feeling of enthusiasm for good things in other people.

29. When speaking with others, I attempt to look at things through their point of view as well as my own.

30. I am now genuinely interested in other people.

31. I wear a sincere, heartwarming smile everywhere I go. My genuine smile comes from deep within my innermost being.

32. I remember the names of other people easily and effortlessly.

33. I encourage other people to talk about themselves and I listen intently.

34. When I speak to others, I focus on their interests not mine.

35. When I need someone to do something, I make them feel happy to do it by pointing out the benefits to them.

36. I sincerely recognize the value in every person I meet and make a genuine effort to make them feel important.

Dr. Stem
Be Encouraged

IF YOU WANT TO FLY WITH THE EAGLES, YOU HAVE TO STOP SWIMMING WITH THE DUCKS.

Loving & Romantic Love

Deep inside you... there's a person who refuses to be kept deep inside you.

Anonymous

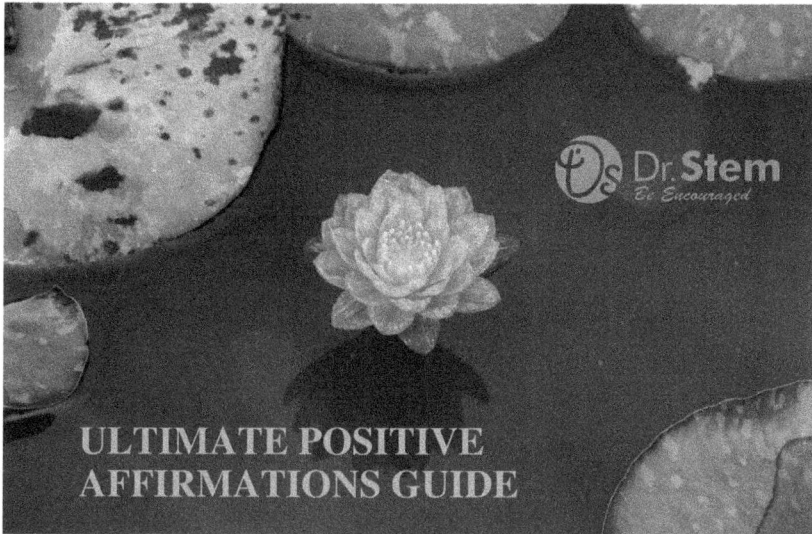

ULTIMATE POSITIVE
AFFIRMATIONS GUIDE

1. I am always faithful to my spouse in my thoughts and in my actions.

2. I am now in total spiritual and physical harmony with the love of my life.

3. I now create feelings of spiritual connection toward my lover.

4. I now create a romantic, loving environment for myself and my lover on a regular basis.

5. I am now consumed with love and affection towards my spouse.

6. I am now a tender and loving lover.

7. I now create romantic magic and loving moments for my lover every day.

8. I softly and sensually touch my lover easily and often.

9. I create feelings of love and passion towards the love of my life every day. I now create these feelings in my body.

10. My subconscious mind now doubles my physical pleasure every time I am touched by my lover.

11. My touch now transfers love, tenderness, and spiritual energy to my lover.

12. I am now loving my spouse the way they want to be loved. I am focused on their need for love.

13. Our love is filled with endless variety and ecstasy.

14. When I love my spouse, I give myself over to feelings of love and passion easily and completely.

15. All my internal images of my lover are big, bright, beautiful, and loving.

16. I am now gentle and sensitive to the needs of my lover.

17. When I love my spouse, I am totally relaxed and comfortable.

18. I am now clean, slim, and sexy. I take care of my body so that I will be most pleasing to the love of my life.

19. My spouse now finds me incredibly attractive and pleasing.

20. I think of little things to please the love of my life daily.

21. All of my conversations with my spouse are now filled with peace, love, and harmony.

22. I am now a fun and playful lover. Our love life is filled with excitement and variety.

23. Every cell in my being is sensitive to my lover's touch.

24. I am always kind, loving, compassionate, and forgiving to the love of my life.

25. I am now open and honest with my spouse every day.

26. I intensify my emotional feelings towards my lover every day. I now feel these feelings in the core of my being.

27. I now know what pleases my lover and I do it with love and with skill.

28. I now touch my lover in exactly the way they want to be touched.

29. I am insatiably curious about new ways to love my spouse.

30. My spouse and I now create secret, romantic interludes on a regular basis to add variety to our love life.

31. I daydream about my lover throughout the day, every day.

32. I am now filled with energy and excitement.

33. I now fulfill all the needs of the love of my life.

34. I treat my lover as if they are the most important person in the world to me.

35. I now treat my lover the way I want them to treat me.

36. I now pamper my lover with all the good feelings and things in life. Our life together is magical.

37. I find new ways to regularly create romantic surprises for my lover.

Affirmations For Couples & Marriage

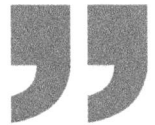

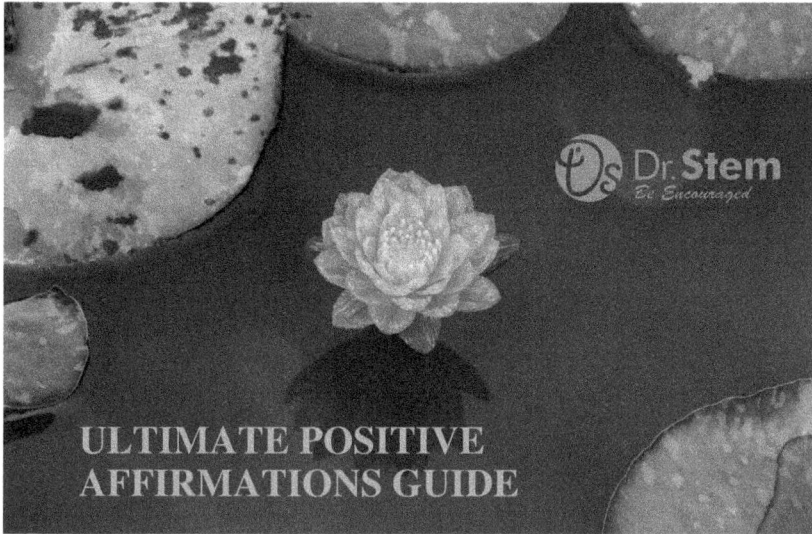

ULTIMATE POSITIVE
AFFIRMATIONS GUIDE

1. Our lines of communications are always open and always open to change.

2. I love you as you are.

3. I take responsibility for my words and actions.

4. I forgive when necessary and I apologize when necessary.

5. My respect and trust are unwavering.

6. I am enjoying the things in my marriage that I already have and make me happy.

7. I appreciate my spouse for all he/she does for our marriage.

8. My spouse and I decide daily to love each other.

9. I am daily making my relationship with my spouse stronger.

10. I choose to listen to my spouse before speaking out of anger.

11. I accept the opportunity to apologize first.

12. I am both loyal and devoted to my spouse.

13. I support my spouse in his/her decisions.

14. Together we have great strengths.

15. We live a live full of gratefulness.

16. Each day is an opportunity to learn more about my spouse.

17. I respect the person my spouse is, rather than who I want him/her to be.

18. I choose to focus on the positive... every day.

19. My marriage is built on love, respect, and trust.

20. We freely accept each other's differences without judgement.

21. I love my spouse unconditionally.

22. There are open lines of communication every day.

23. I give my spouse space to become him/herself within the confines of our marriage.

24. We laugh together on a regular basis.

25. Our marriage is growing stronger every day.

26. I understand that we will have bad days, but we get up and carry on... together.

27. I must forgive my spouse... daily.

28. I am irresistible to my spouse and will not deny him when possible.

29. I will ask myself regularly, "How can I show him/her my love more? "

30. Together there is nothing we cannot face or triumph over.

31. My spouse is... and will always be...my best friend.

32. I must control my tongue when angry and fight fair if we should disagree.

33. I yearn to kiss my spouse daily... morning and night.

34. I am passionate in my love for my spouse.

35. My marriage is a match made in heaven.

36. I believe in my marriage.

37. I celebrate my marriage.

38. I accept that my spouse and I are different... and respect those differences.

39. Communication must be open and honest.

40. I will be patient and kind. I will not envy, or boast, or be proud. I will not dishonor others, or be self-seeking, or easily angered, nor will I keep a record of wrongs. I will not delight in evil, but I will rejoice in the truth. I will always protect, always trust, always hope, always persevere. I know love never fails. (1 Corinthians 13:4-8)

41. He/she is the love of my life... and honestly completes me in nearly every way (no matter how cliché it sounds).

42. He/she teaches me more about myself than I could ever have learned on my own.

43. He/she gives me compassion and empathy when needed and has taught me to give them back to him.

44. He /she totally gets it when it comes to romance. He playfully flirts with me... daily... and often.

45. Even when he hasn't got a clue, he tries so hard. And at everything. He then becomes simply irresistible to me.

Dr. Stem
Be Encouraged

Affirmations For Parents
& Parents-To-Be

Success is not just about what you accomplish in life; it's about what you inspire others to do.

Unknown

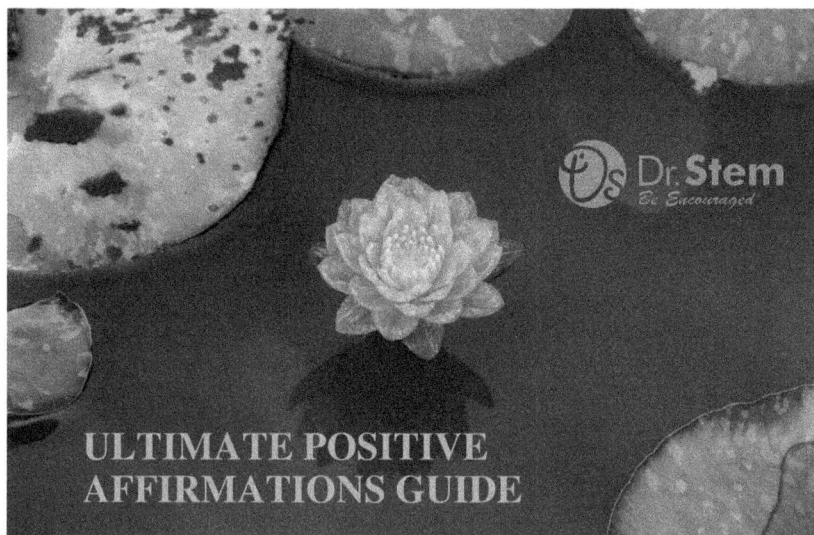

ULTIMATE POSITIVE
AFFIRMATIONS GUIDE

1. I am a great parent.

2. I am going to be a great parent.

3. I am aware of my child's nature and supportive of them living their truth.

4. I am willing to learn and grow.

5. I am grateful for the resources that continue to show up to help me be a great parent.

6. My spouse and I agree on healthy parenting approaches.

7. Our home is a place of peace.

8. We enjoy each other's company and know when to give each other privacy.

9. Our home is orderly and organized.

10. Everyone is willing to contribute to maintaining the order and function of our home.

11. My children do their chores willingly.

12. I know how to support their true natures by giving them jobs they can accomplish easily.

13. We have a lot of fun in our home.

14. We are making fond memories with the activities we enjoy in our home.

15. I love the traditions we have that support our day-to-day and holiday experiences.

16. When something is out of balance, I prayerfully seek answers and am led to solutions that make a difference.

17. I am confident and growing in my parenting role.

18. I listen to the spirit and I am guided.

19. I do what is correct for me and my children.

20. I support others in choosing the same.

21. Comparisons do not serve me; I notice when I compare myself to other parents and I quickly let them go.

22. I love being a parent.

23. I love how much joy this role gives me.

24. I am healthy and vibrant.

25. I take the time I need to care for my own needs; doing this supports me in being a better parent.

26. I get the rest I need.

27. I easily make changes when change is the best option.

28. It's amazing how successful our family is.

29. We have a great time together.

30. I am grateful

Affirmations To Help Heal A Broken Heart After Breakup or Betrayal

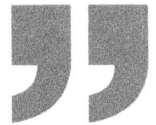

Keep your head up. God gives his hardest battles to his strongest soldiers.

Unknown

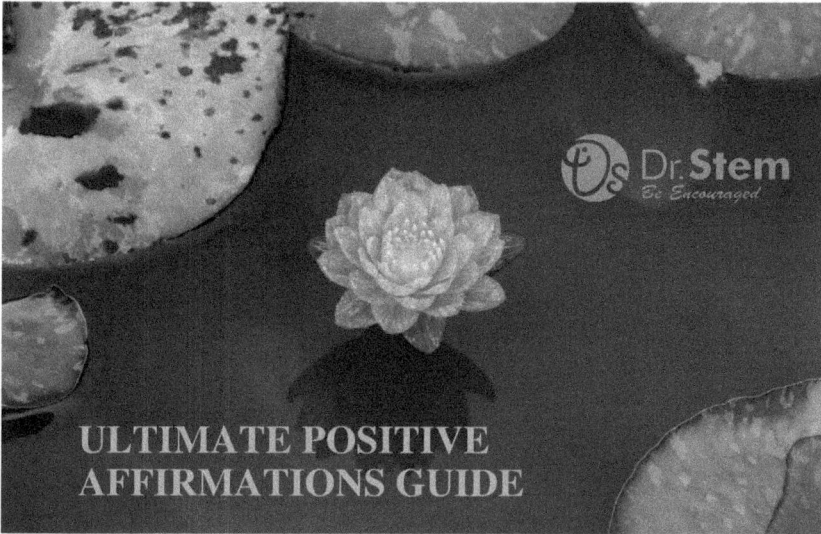

ULTIMATE POSITIVE
AFFIRMATIONS GUIDE

1. I am a being of love

2. I am loved and lovable

3. I forgive myself

4. I forgive my ex

5. I have power over my own life

6. My wounds are healing

7. I am deserving of love

8. I am releasing the past

9. I am learning to trust myself

10. There is something better waiting for me

11. I am whole on my own

12. I matter

13. I am excited about this new beginning

14. I am capable of loving again

15. I am learning to love myself unconditionally

16. It is getting easier day by day

17. I am enough

18. I have a lot to offer

19. I am becoming stronger

20. Everything is unfolding as it is supposed to

21. I honor the love I shared

22. I can find happiness in any situation

23. I am grateful for the lessons

24. I am excited to start my new life

25. I choose happiness, health, and harmony

26. I enjoy spending time with myself

27. I am free to be the best version of me

28. I am likable, lovable, and worthy of love

29. I am finding peace

30. I am allowing myself to feel joy, laugh, and smile

31. I am working on me, for me

32. I am allowing myself to feel all my emotions

33. My heart is opening up to new possibilities

34. I am capable of trusting again

35. I attract positive and healthy relationships

36. This is just a small part of my story

37. I am learning to trust the process

38. I know I have worth and value

39. I am healing more and more every day

40. I am allowing myself to let go

41. I am an attractive person

42. I will open my heart when I am ready

43. I give all relationships my all

44. I am loved

45. I am worthy of love even when my heart is hurting.

46. I am a loving, peaceful, joyful person. I am loved and lovable.

47. This break-up is the beginning of a positive new direction in my life.

48. I choose to break free from negativity.

49. Love, forgive, and move on.

50. Even though I may miss some things about my ex and my relationship, I am happier and healthier being single.

51. My life is perfect just the way it is.

52. I forgive my ex.

53. Everything is unfolding as it is supposed to.

54. I am healing more and more every day.

55. I am not a burden and it's not selfish for me to nourish myself in whatever way I need.

56. I don't need anyone else to make me happy.

57. I find strength through my struggle and trust my greatness.

58. Each day in every way I am peaceful, healed, happy, and whole.

59. I choose happiness, health, and harmony instead of dis-functional relationships.

60. I am connected to so many people around me, and they don't mind taking care of me right now.

61. I would rather be healthy and single than in a relationship that is unhealthy.

62. Having risked opening my heart to love. I choose to live in love in every moment.

63. Never ever give up on your dreams or your perfect life.

64. I will get through this. This did not end me.

65. I did my best. I am trying my best. I am doing what I need to be doing.

66. I love myself. I love my life Love is all there is.

67. I love myself and my life and I am worthy of love in my life.

68. It is completely normal that I am upset or devastated over this breakup.

69. It's OK to not be OK. It's OK to take the time and space I need to heal.

70. I am strong, resilient, peaceful, and happy.

71. I am loving and compassionate to myself at all times.

72. All of me is good and lovable. I can be all of myself at all times.

73. It's OK to think about my ex, to question what happened, and to replay every detail in my head. But eventually, I will move on.

74. I am infinitely deserving of love.

75. I do not measure my worth on this breakup.

76. I will be better than I've ever been before.

77. This happened for a reason.

78. I will love again.

79. I will not only think about all the great things from that relationship.

ONE DAY
AS AN EAGLE
IS BETTER THAN A
THOUSAD AS
A TURKEY

Dr. Stem
Be Encouraged

Affirmations For Divorcing and Divorced Women

What you get by achieving your goals is not as important as what you become in pursuing those goals.

— Henry David Thoreau

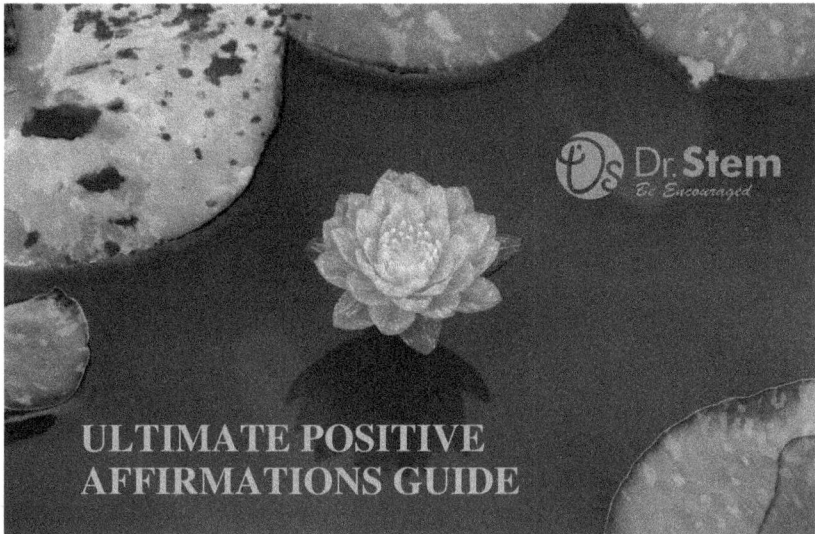

ULTIMATE POSITIVE
AFFIRMATIONS GUIDE

1. Everything is happening as it should be.

2. I am grateful for the relationship I had with my former partner.

3. I learned a lot about myself in my past relationship.

4. Relationships are an opportunity for me to learn and grow

5. I choose to be happy and hopeful even though it may seem too difficult.

6. It's ok to feel lost at times this is only a temporary situation.

7. I am still the same beautiful and attractive woman I was when I first got married.

8. I will calmly observe my emotions with complete mindfulness.

9. These affirmations will help me make better choices in my life.

10. I am a work in progress and am constantly improving.

11. I'm ok with my divorce.

12. There's no reason to be embarrassed or ashamed of my divorce.

13. I forgive myself for all the hurtful things I said and did out of anger to my ex.

14. I forgive my ex for all the hurtful things he said and did out of anger.

15. I will avoid putting the blame on him because I realize we both had our faults.

16. I am capable of making healthy decisions for my personal and spiritual evolvement.

17. I have a bright future ahead of me.

18. Divorce is not the end of the road.

19. Change is the only constant, and I will move through this with grace and ease.

20. I have an opportunity now to create the life I want.

21. Creating a new life is an exciting opportunity.

22. I am a strong and independent woman, and I don't need a man to complete my life.

23. My heart is healing.

24. I am fully capable of being alone right now and I'm ok with it.

25. I am a good person with a lot to offer.

Affirmations For Divorcing and Divorced Men

Concentration is the ability to think absolutely nothing when it's absolutely necessary

— Ray Knight

ULTIMATE POSITIVE
AFFIRMATIONS GUIDE

1. I know that everything will be okay.

2. Everything in life happens for the perfect reason.

3. I am grateful for what I learned in my past relationship.

4. I release and let go of all anger and resentment towards my ex.

5. I am ok with being on my own.

6. I am excited to create a new life for myself.

7. I welcome change into my life.

8. Divorce is not the end of the road. It's a new beginning.

9. My happiness does not rely on being with someone else.

10. I am a sexy, handsome, and strong man.

11. I choose to focus on the positive aspects of my ex-partner.

12. I accept the divorce and I accept my ex for who she is.

13. Everything in life happens for the perfect reason.

14. I am grateful for what I learned in my past relationship.

15. I release and let go of all anger and resentment towards my ex.

16. I am ok with being on my own.

17. I am excited to create a new life for myself.

18. I welcome change into my life.

19. Divorce is not the end of the road. It's a new beginning.

20. My happiness does not rely on being with someone else.

21. I choose to focus on the positive aspects of my former partner.

22. I accept the divorce and I accept my ex for who she is.

23. I forgive myself for all the hurtful things I've said and did out of anger to my ex.

24. I forgive my ex for all the hurtful things she said and did to me out of anger.

25. I release and let go of all blame because I understand we both had our faults that contributed to the divorce.

26. I let go of feelings of hate, anger, and bitterness towards my ex.

27. I am open to change and embrace the new opportunities that will come into my life now.

28. I am open to meeting new people when the time is right.

29. Even though I lost someone I still have a lot of love to give.

30. There is nothing to be embarrassed about. Not everything in life works out the way we hope for and that's ok.

31. My future looks bright. I have a lot to look forward to now.

32. I am not a failure.

33. I am not alone. I am grateful for the friends and family I have.

34. I am a good person with a lot to offer.

35. I deserve good people in my life.

Daily Affirmations Recovering From A Narcissistic Relationship

What counts can't always be counted; what can be counted doesn't always count.

—— Albert Einstein

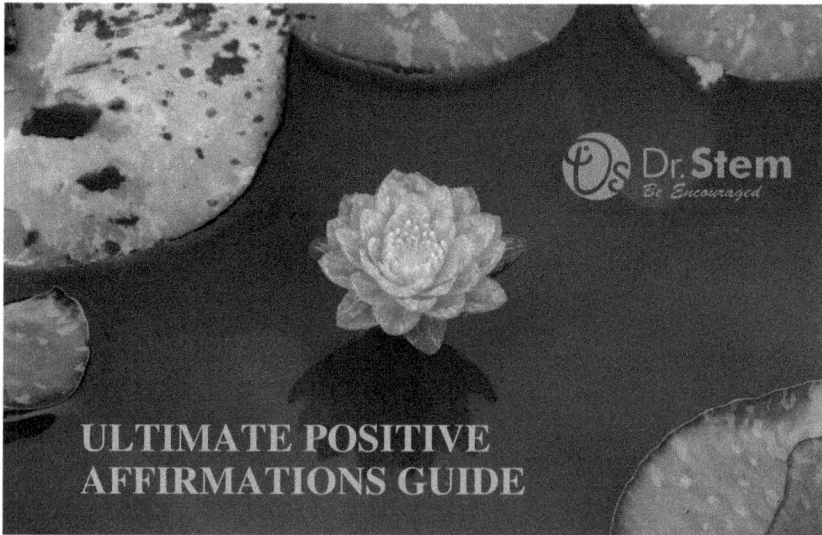

ULTIMATE POSITIVE
AFFIRMATIONS GUIDE

1. I do not deserve abuse.

2. I am a good and kind person.

3. I am talented and have many things to offer

4. I actively contribute to my healing.

5. I enjoy making others laugh.

6. I am an excellent listener.

7. I have many supportive friends who help me.

8. I liberate myself from this unhealthy relationship.

9. I am a loyal friend and partner.

10. I empathize with others.

Affirmations For Anxiety, Depression & Becoming Peaceful

Amateurs think about short-cuts and success. Professionals think about daily habits and making progress.

—— Maxime Legace

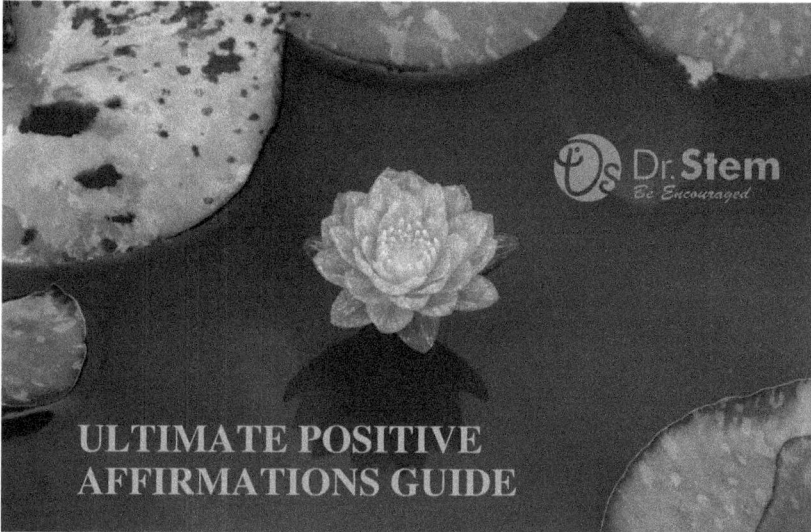

ULTIMATE POSITIVE AFFIRMATIONS GUIDE

1. I choose to feel calm.

2. I choose positive and nurturing thoughts.

3. I am right where I need to be.

4. I do the best that I can.

5. I forgive myself.

6. I release the past.

7. I look forward to a happy bright future.

8. I am safe.

9. I inhale the good and exhale the bad. (variations on this include... I inhale energy/light/health and I exhale negativity/darkness/illness. Often this affirmation can be used with meditation and certain yoga poses)

10. I am brave/I am strong.

11. I will be OK.

12. I am not my anxiety.

13. I am not my depression

14. I am currently reducing my anxiety.

15. I am currently reducing my sadness and emptiness

16. I choose to seek professional help so that I can feel better

17. I focus my energy on my values, not my anxiety.

18. I focus my energy on values not my depression.

19. I have the strength to move beyond my anxiety.

20. I have strength to move beyond my depression.

21. I am in charge of my breathing.

22. I am peace.

23. I am love.

24. I cultivate inner calm.

25. I appreciate the beauty around me.

26. I will survive. (I have survived my anxiety before. I will survive now)

27. I will survive.

28. I am curious about my triggers.

29. I am patient.

30. I take things one step at a time/I take things one day at a time.

31. I am present in this moment.

32. I am not in danger; I am just uncomfortable; this too will pass.

33. My breath is calm and relaxed.

34. I now have energy to be and do what I love.

35. I am at peace when I am around others

36. I enjoy the light

37. I enjoy getting up and doing something I enjoy every day

38. My mind is at peace.

39. Everything is going to be okay.

40. I am in control of my thoughts.

41. I choose to think positively.

42. I am calm and at peace.

43. I am letting go of my stress.

44. I feel my stress melting away.

45. I release any stress related thoughts.

46. I am free from stress.

47. I am peaceful and centered.

48. I feel the stress slowly leaving my body.

49. My mind and body are relaxed and calm.

50. I choose to live in peace.

Affirmations For Overcoming Grief

So many others before you have changed their life for the better. **Why not you?**

Anonymous

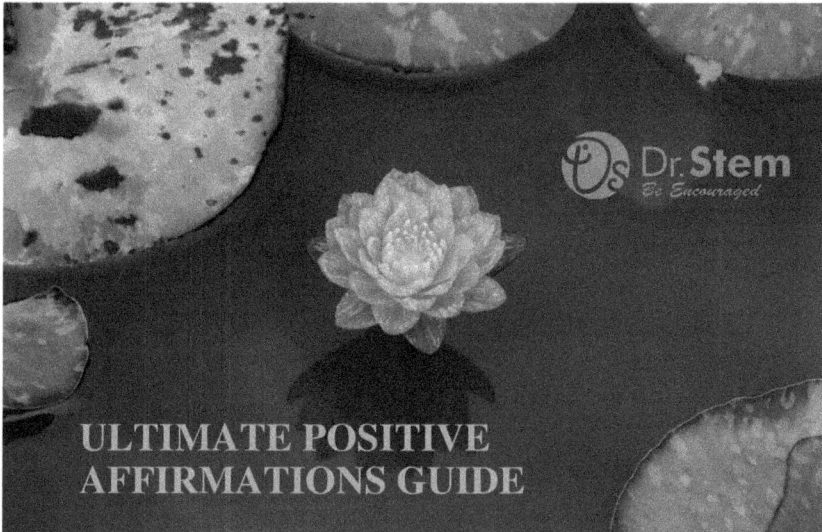

ULTIMATE POSITIVE
AFFIRMATIONS GUIDE

1. I release the tension in my body and relax.

2. I allow myself to feel my grief and then let go.

3. I can focus on being productive today.

4. I take comfort in the memories of my loved one.

5. I recognize painful moments, but I know it will pass.

6. I will hold on to love and release the grief.

7. I can feel happy and hopeful today.

8. I choose to feel the presence of my loved one.

9. I give myself time and space to feel all my feelings.

10. I will give myself a break today.

11. I can be gentle with myself as I heal.

12. My heart feels lighter today.

13. It's okay that I need time to grieve.

14. I will take the time to care for my needs today.

15. It's okay to feel overwhelmed but I will feel better soon.

16. I can cope with the grieving process.

17. I can ask for help if I need it.

18. I will accomplish my goals today.

19. I feel grateful for all the love in my life.

20. I choose to feel at peace today.

21. I acknowledge that In my grief, I have changed

22. Death does not break the bond of love

23. I can hold on to love and let go of grief

24. My focus is on my blessings

25. Everything must come to an end

26. Everyone's life has meaning I embrace that.

27. The pain in my heart will heal

28. I'm not angry. I'm grieving

29. It's ok for me to take time to grieve

30. Grief reminds me that I'm alive

31. I am never alone in my grief

32. In my grief I am loved

33. In my brief I love myself

Affirmations For Self-Discipline

Success is not just about what you accomplish in life; it's about what you inspire others to do.

Unknown

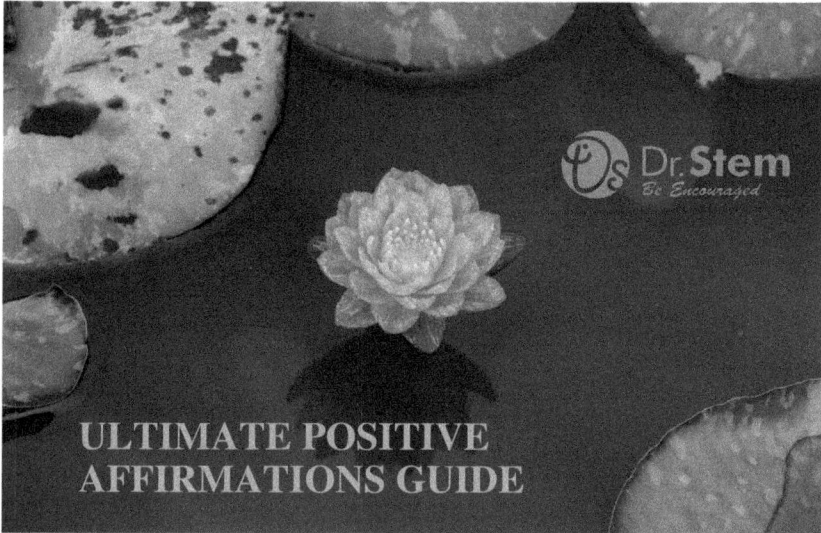

ULTIMATE POSITIVE
AFFIRMATIONS GUIDE

1. Every day my discipline is improving more.

2. I have a dedicated and focused mindset.

3. I am in control of my actions.

4. I find it easy to maintain focus and clarity.

5. I can control my impulses.

6. I am a highly disciplined person.

7. Nothing will stop me from getting what I want.

8. Every day I am attracting everything I desire in life.

9. I will do whatever it takes to reach my highest potential.

10. There is nothing and no one that can stop me from doing what I strive for.

11. I welcome challenges and will persist through the hard times.

12. I realize there will be obstacles, but I have the strength to get through them.

13. I have an unshakeable perseverance.

14. I can accomplish anything I set my mind to.

15. I have a focused mind that is clear of distracting thoughts.

16. I can tackle any project with effort and ease.

17. Focusing on tasks comes naturally to me.

18. I am willing and able to get things done on time.

19. My focus is sharp and disciplined.

20. Nothing distracts me.

21. I am focused.

22. I am productive and I pay close attention to detail.

23. I find it easy to direct my attention on important tasks and not get distracted.

24. I work diligently every day and set goals for myself.

25. I am consistent in my disciplinary habits.

26. I am disciplined.

Dr. Stem
Be Encouraged

Self-discipline
begins with the mastery
of your thoughts.
If you don't control
what you think,
you can't control
what you do.

Affirmations For Doing What You Love

Talent in itself means nothing; while experience, acquired in humility and with hard work means everything.

Unknown

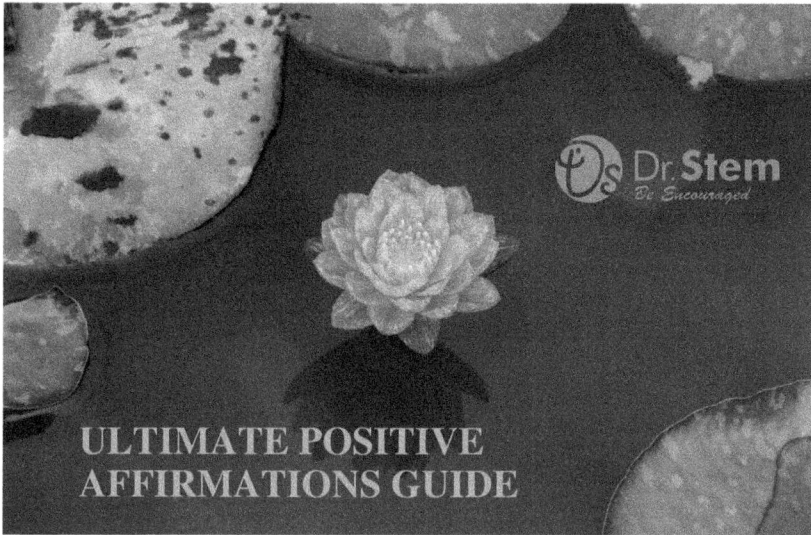

ULTIMATE POSITIVE
AFFIRMATIONS GUIDE

1. I am confident and able to handle any obstacle thrown in front of me.

2. My presence is my power.

3. I am superior to negative thoughts and low actions.

4. I treat others with respect and appreciate their individuality.

5. I have the power to create positive change.

6. My ability to conquer my challenges is limitless; my potential to succeed is infinite.

7. I am focused and persistent.

8. I am in the process of becoming the best version of myself.

9. I am grateful to learn from new experiences, even if I struggle.

10. I am proud of myself and all that I have accomplished.

11. I am unique and my ability to manifest my intended level of greatness depends upon that uniqueness.

12. I am doing what I love.

13. I can never be comfortable living below my potential.

14. There is an action for every problem.

15. The more I give, the more I receive.

16. I make decisions quickly and I keep my methods flexible.

17. I communication to achieve a desired result not to simply deliver information.

18. I presuppose the life I want daily.

19. I am different, that is my unique selling proposition.

20. I am a people person.

21. I am willing to make the sacrifices necessary to accomplish the results I want.

22. I am always improving.

23. I think and act according to my moral compass.

24. I was created to do those things that are the most challenging.

25. I care more than others think is wise.

26. I risk more than others think is safe.

27. I dream bigger than others think is practical.

28. I expect more than others think is possible.

29. I do good unto others.

30. I am proactive.

31. I maintain a positive outlook on life.

Affirmations For
Never Giving Up

Keep your face to the sunshine and you can never see the shadow.

Helen Keller

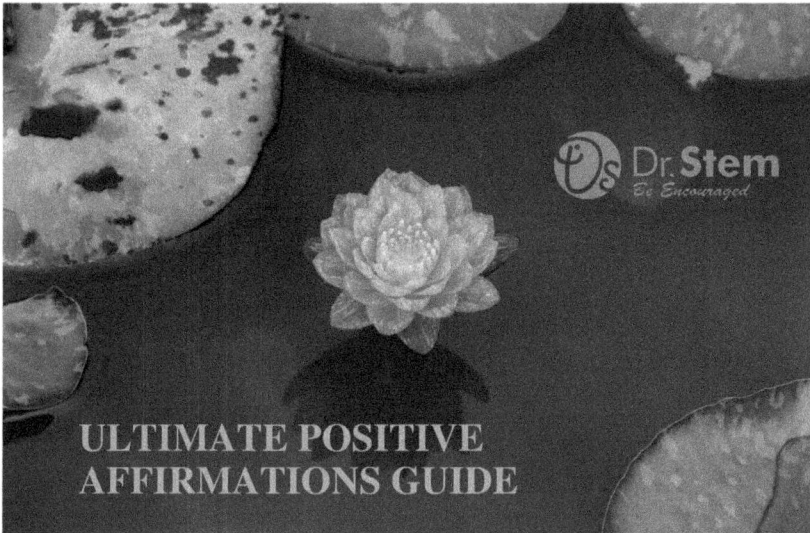

ULTIMATE POSITIVE
AFFIRMATIONS GUIDE

1. I will never quit.

2. Failure is not an option.

3. I am a survivor.

4. I am in control of my destiny.

5. I will keep moving forward.

6. I am fully committed to my goals and objectives.

7. I am determined to achieve great things in my life and won't stop until I get it.

8. I release all negative programming of self-doubts and fears that keep me from moving forward.

9. No matter how hard it gets, I will never surrender.

10. I am so close to my goals; I will not give up.

11. I am a magnet for success.

12. I feel accomplished when I reach a goal.

13. I know that hard work pays off and I am fully committed.

14. Progress and effort are all that matters.

15. I don't participate in leisure activities until my work goals have been met.

16. I set goals every day and strive to achieve them.

17. Focusing on my goals gives me something to work towards.

18. I have good work habits.

19. I am patient.

WHEN A STORM IS COMING, ALL OTHER BIRDS SEEK SHELTER. THE EAGLE ALONE AVOIDS THE STORM BY FLYING ABOVE IT. BE AN EAGLE.

Dr. Stem
Be Encouraged

Daily Affirmations for Work & Business Stress

The best work that anybody ever writes is the work that is on the verge of embarrassing him always.

Arthur Miller

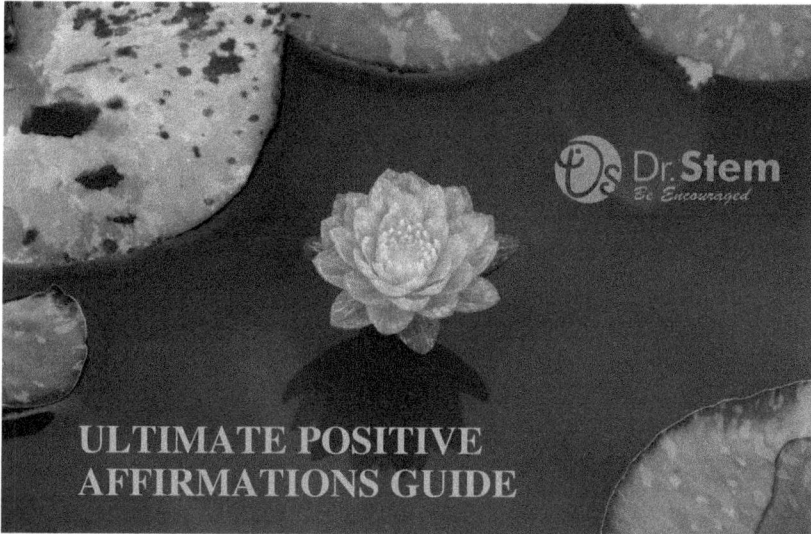

ULTIMATE POSITIVE
AFFIRMATIONS GUIDE

1. I choose to release my work -business stress.

2. I feel calm and balanced at my work

3. I feel calm and balanced in my business

4. I act peacefully even in stressful work, business situations.

5. I can control how my work, business affects me.

6. Feeling calm at my work comes easily to me.

7. Feeling calm in my business comes easily.

8. I am surrounded by positive and peaceful co-workers.

9. I am surrounded by positive business colleagues and customers.

10. I am letting go of my fears and anxieties.

11. I am calm and relaxed

12. I am free from stress

13. I can feel stress melting away

14. I am centered and at peace

15. I love myself the way I am.

16. I deserve to be happy and successful.

17. I choose a peaceful and stress-free life.

18. I am in control of my life.

19. I am at peace.

20. Everything is going to be okay.

21. I choose to be positive and confident.

22. Stress and work pressure have no place in my life.

23. I choose to address stress from a calm and peaceful place.

24. My mind is clear, and I am thinking with clarity.

25. My body is relaxed, and I sense tension dissolving.

26. I exhale stress and inhale calmness.

27. As my breathing gets slower and deeper, I sense tension flowing out of my mind.

28. I am letting go of my fears and worries with slow and deliberate deep breaths.

29. Pressure situations bring out the best in me.

30. I took up a demanding job as a challenge.

31. Challenges are just opportunities to prove my worth.

32. I sense love and support from my colleagues.

33. I am a team player and can get along well with others.

34. I feel comfortable interacting and working with people.

35. I get credited for skill and effort at work.

36. I love my job and enjoy working with team members.

37. I am calm and in control at work.

38. I am adept at handling any situation.

39. I am talented enough to complete the work on time.

40. Nothing can upset or overwhelm me.

41. One day at a time, one step at a time.

42. I am grateful for the opportunities and rewards of my job.

43. I am calm and relaxed in pressure situations.

44. I am releasing the negative energy from my body.

45. My life is heading in the right direction.

46. Asking for help is not a sign of failure.

47. Good things happen naturally to me.

48. Happy and relaxed is my normal state of mind.

49. I am confident about my life and my abilities.

50. I forgive myself for the mistakes committed in the past.

51. Every mistake is an opportunity to learn.

52. This too shall pass. For every low, there is a high.

53. There are things I can't change or have no control over. I am okay with that.

54. There is no hurdle I cannot get the better of when I put my mind to it.

55. A situation is neither good nor bad. It just is.

56. I choose to react positively to any situation I come across.

57. My past cannot prevent me from succeeding now or in the future.

58. It is okay to make mistakes.

59. I have everything within my grasp to be successful.

60. I deserve respect and recognition.

61. I accept myself with all my flaws and I don't feel the need for approval.

62. My mistakes do not define me or my future performances.

63. I am brimming with energy and ready to face the day.

64. I try to give my best in everything I do.

65. I respect myself and deserve respect from others.

66. I can do this as well as anybody else.

67. I bring a positive attitude to work every day.

68. My team respects and values my contribution.

69. Every day I am learning to become a better me.

Affirmations for
Breaking Bad Habbits

*Work for something because it's good; not just
because it stands a chance to succeed.*

— Vaclav Havel

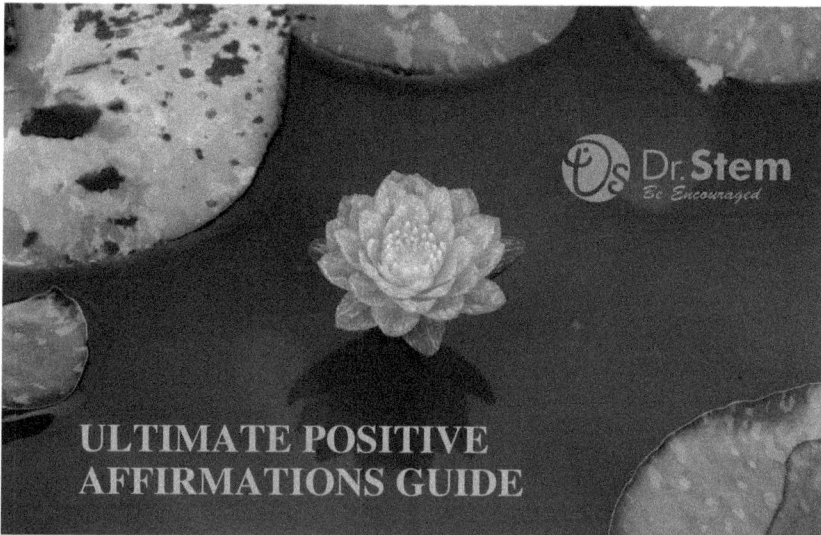

ULTIMATE POSITIVE
AFFIRMATIONS GUIDE

1. All habits in my life are health-giving.

2. All my habits are positive and beneficial.

3. All my habits support me in positive ways.

4. Changing my behavior is as easy as changing my thoughts.

5. Day by day, I am gaining more control over my past habits.

6. Each time a challenge a past habit, I feel a greater sense of control and self-esteem.

7. Every day I am developing new and positive habits.

8. I always do what is best for my body.

9. I always exercise discretion in all that I do.

10. I am always adding positive new rituals to my daily routine.

11. I am calmly and confidently letting go of...

12. I am changing my habits by changing my thoughts.

13. I am changing my life for the better.

14. I am cleansing myself from all past habits.

15. I am completely committed to living a life free from...

16. I am finally free!

17. I am forever grateful to finally be free from...

18. I am free from the control of addictions.

19. I am in charge of my behaviors and actions.

20. I am in complete control of all the habits in my life.

21. I am in control of every aspect of my life.

22. I am in control of my life.

23. I am incredibly proud of myself for finally giving up...

24. I am the master of my habits.

25. I control all my impulses.

26. I am learning to override past habitual behaviors.

27. I am learning to take control of my habits.

28. I am now free from all obsessions.

29. I am now free from...

30. I am strong enough to overcome any habit.

31. I am stronger than any addiction.

32. I am stronger than any habit.

33. I am the master of my mind and body.

34. I am very proud of my healthy lifestyle.

35. I break bad habits by making them less enjoyable to do.

36. I choose to let go of my attachment to past habits.

37. I choose to live a healthy life.

38. I conquer bad habits by learning their purpose and creating new habits that address this even better.

39. I consciously interrupt and reprogram all habitual behaviors.

40. I constantly examine my habits, and change those that no longer serve me.

41. I control my habitual actions by eliminating habitual thoughts.

42. I control habitual reactions by exercising conscious thinking.

43. I create new positive habits by practicing them every day without fail.

44. I create new self-empowering habits every day.

45. I do things differently at every opportunity.

46. I easily ignore habitual cravings.

47. I easily let go of old routines so that I can embrace more empowering ones.

48. I easily move away from negative habits.

49. I easily overcome negative habits.

50. I easily relieve stress and tension without the need for habitual crutches.

51. I easily resist the temptation to return to old habits.

52. I eliminate disempowering habits quickly and easily.

53. I ensure that all my habits are positive and empowering.

54. I feel great about my healthy new habits.

55. I form new, positive habits every day.

56. I gratefully let go of old, limiting behaviors.

57. I have all the resolve I need to make positive changes in my life.

58. I have complete control over my actions.

59. I have complete control over my impulses.

60. I have identified all my bad habits and am taking daily steps to curtail them.

61. I have incredible self-control.

62. I have now conquered the habit of...

63. I have now gained control over my past need to...

64. I have the willpower to live a healthy life.

65. I hold the power of change in my mind.

66. I honor my body in every way.

67. I know all urges and impulses will pass with time

68. I know that change is never a loss... it is only change.

69. I let all urges pass by accepting them for what they are and watching them fade away.

70. I love creating positive new ways of being.

71. I maintain healthy, life-empowering habits every day.

72. I only engage in habits that support my well-being.

73. I only get hooked on empowering habits.

74. I only spend my money on positive, life-sustaining habits.

75. I only use food to satisfy legitimate hunger.

76. I prefer vitamins over alcohol.

77. I release all habits that are disempowering.

78. I replace all limiting habits with healthy, empowering ones.

79. I resist all temptations and stick to my new way of being.

80. I step out of my established comfort zone at every opportunity.

81. It feels amazing to finally be free from the need to...

82. It feels good to be taking control of my life and health.

83. It feels great to finally be taking control of my life.

84. My determination is stronger than any habit.

85. My willpower is stronger than any habit.

86. Today I cultivate new, health-sustaining habits.

87. Today I find a better way of being.

88. Today I let go of negative habits.

89. Today I take back control of my life.

90. Week by week I am changing my habits for the better.

Affirmations For Adversity, Affliction & Tough Times

Don't pay attention to what they write about you.
Just measure it in inches.

Andy Warhol

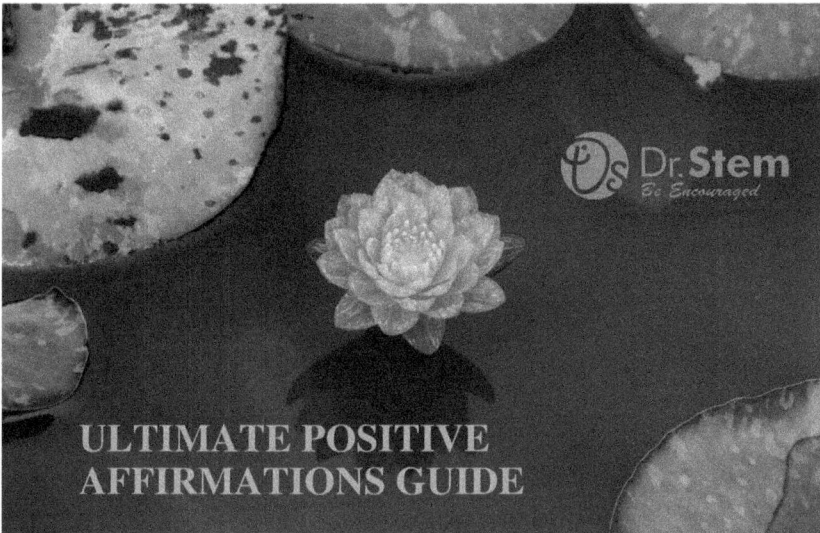

ULTIMATE POSITIVE AFFIRMATIONS GUIDE

1. I can get through anything.

2. There are no problems, only challenges.

3. I welcome challenges into my life.

4. Challenges are opportunities to learn and grow.

5. I am safe and secure no matter what.

6. I can get through anything.

7. I am getting stronger every day.

8. Even in the presence of adversity, I embrace new challenges.

9. I increase my potential for success in the future, when I learn from my mistakes,

10. I am proud of my ability to recover from mistakes.

11. The more I stumble, the more I pick myself up, the easier it becomes to recover.

12. Adversity drives me forward

13. My sense of persistence is reinforced.

14. When I encounter missteps, I become more resolved,

15. I grow more confident, stronger, and less afraid of whatever awaits me

16. Resilience takes conscious practice and commitment.

17. When others give up easily, I now find it difficult to quit.

18. I happily confront new obstacles.

19. I confidently enlist the help of those around me, so we can face the challenges together.

...but they that wait for The LORD
shall renew their strength;
they shall mount up with wings
like eagles. They Shall run
and not be weary;
they shall walk and not faint.
Isaiah 40:31

Affirmations For
Financial Worries

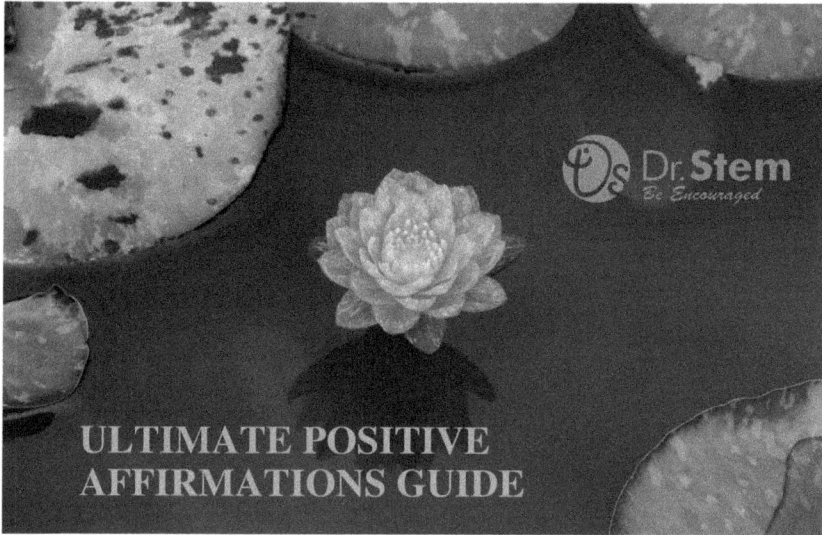

**ULTIMATE POSITIVE
AFFIRMATIONS GUIDE**

1. I attract financial abundance into my life.

2. Money comes to me effortlessly.

3. My bills are paid, and I will live freely.

4. I earn plenty of money and love what I do.

5. I deserve a prosperous life.

6. Money is a tool that can change my life for the better.

7. I control money, money doesn't control me.

8. Money flows to me freely as I move through this world.

9. I can use money to create a better life.

10. My finances don't scare me because I have a plan.

11. I am worthy of a solid financial foundation.

12. Money can expand the opportunities of my life.

13. Negative emotions about money don't serve my financial goals.

14. I am a very capable person that can tackle all money obstacles.

15. More money in my bank account doesn't make me a bad person.

16. I am not poor; I am on the path to a wealthy life.

17. I can become financially free.

18. I have the power to be a financially successful person.

19. I have the power to improve my relationship with money.

20. I can find the positive in my money situation.

21. Through thoughtful generosity, more money will flow back to me.

22. I believe in my ability to use the money that comes into my life to meet my financial goals.

23. It is within my power to create a successful financial future.

24. With hard work and creativity, I can build the financial picture that I desire.

25. My life is full of wealth beyond money.

26. My income can exceed my expenses.

27. Money is an abundant resource that I can earn.

28. My income has unlimited potential and money constantly flows to me with ease

29. I accept the flow of money from multiple sources.

30. My hard work will bring me money.

31. I can leverage my skills to bring in more money at any time.

32. I believe in my ability to earn more money.

33. There are countless opportunities to make more money in my life.

34. I deserve the opportunity to negotiate my salary

35. I deserve to be paid a fair wage for my skills and time.

36. My job provides the opportunity to work towards my financial goals.

37. I can use money to change the world for the better.

38. I have enough money to freely enjoy my day-to-day life.

39. I will attain all the riches that I desire with time.

40. I am on my way to becoming wealthy.

Affirmations For Abundance & Wealth

To achieve what 1% of the world's population has, you must be willing to do what the 99% will not dare to do.

Manoj Arora

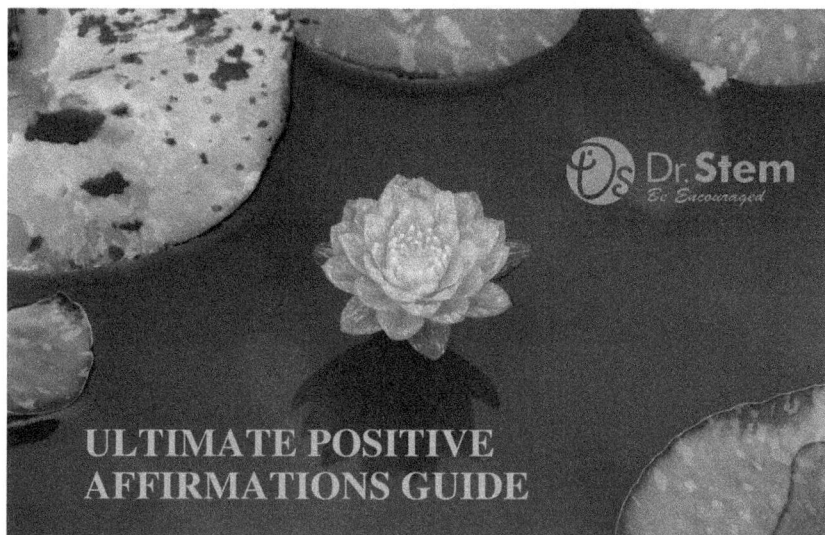

ULTIMATE POSITIVE AFFIRMATIONS GUIDE

1. I am now wealthy.

2. I deserve to be wealthy.

3. I am now a financial genius.

4. I am now highly pleasing to myself in the presence of other people.

5. I now save, spend, and invest my money wisely.

6. My wealth is increasing massively every day.

7. My money is now creating more money.

8. My outstanding ideas, energy, and passion are now creating new wealth for me and others around me.

9. All the investments I own are profitable.

10. I now give away massive amounts of wealth to causes that I believe in.

11. Every dollar I spend returns to me massively multiplied.

12. I manage my money effectively with precision.

13. I now have all the money that I want and need.

14. I now give away large amounts of wealth wisely and intelligently.

15. Every thought I have is now being transformed into massive financial abundance for me.

16. I am now creating all of the wealth that I want and need.

17. My imagination is now creating all the financial abundance that I desire.

18. The more of my wealth that I give away wisely, the more my personal wealth explodes massively.

19. I now seize my opportunities boldly and courageously decisively applying my faith through my actions.

20. My imagination now creates all the wealth I desire.

21. Through my power of intention, I effortlessly attract all the wealth I need and desire.

22. I habitually give more than I get. I cheerfully go the extra mile in every task I undertake.

23. I am now receptive to unexpected gifts of wealth.

24. I am now accumulating vast amounts of wealth consistent with my integrity and honesty.

25. I respectfully accept the gifts of others with the knowledge that these gifts were intended to gratify the giver more than the receiver.

26. I am a gracious giver and receiver.

27. When I think wealthy thoughts, I become wealthier in all aspects of my life.

28. My wealth is now multiplying and creating more wealth easily and effortlessly.

29. My financial abundance is now exploding massively 24 hours a day even when I am playing, eating, and sleeping.

30. I am now surrounded by an ocean of wealth and I draw from this ocean all I need.

31. My job is my personal pipeline from which I tap the infinite wealth from my world economy for my personal desires.

32. I am now earning massive amounts of wealth doing what I love to do while rendering useful service to other people.

33. Through my power of my subconscious mind, I effortlessly attract all the wealth I need and desire.

34. I am a money magnet.

35. Money is forever circulating in my life and there is always a surplus.

36. I have a responsibility to accumulate vast sums of wealth through useful service to others and to give it back to society through gifts that benefit the entire community.

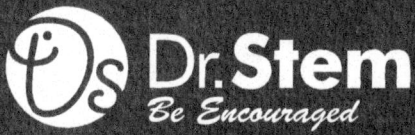
Dr. Stem
Be Encouraged

Affirmations For Budgeting, Saving & Overcoming Debt

Freedom is not the absence of challenges and commitments; but the ability to choose yours.

— Paulo Coelho

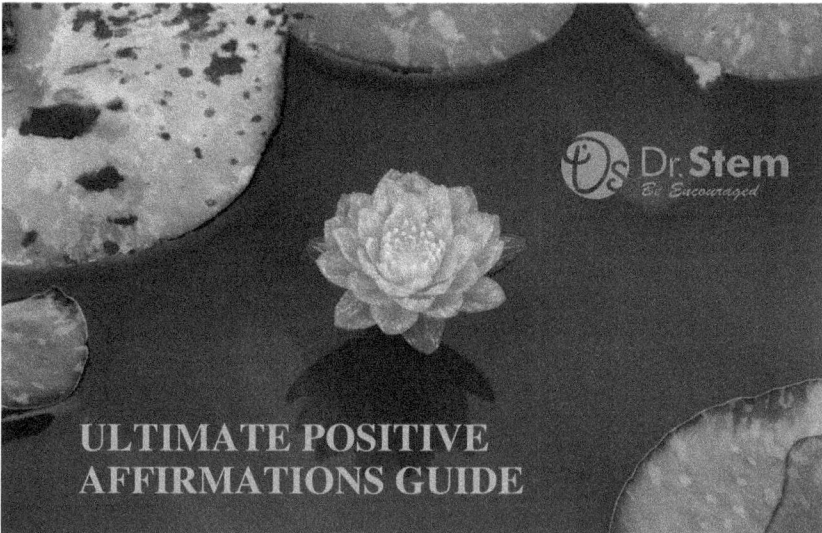

ULTIMATE POSITIVE
AFFIRMATIONS GUIDE

1. I choose to spend my money wisely.

2. I can make my dreams a reality with careful budgeting.

3. Finding ways to have fun in a frugal way is enjoyable.

4. I can track my expenses and stick to a budget.

5. I have the discipline to make hard financial choices now to enjoy an easy life later.

6. My future self will thank me for saving money.

7. I will build an emergency fund to safeguard myself.

8. I am in control of my expenses.

9. I enjoy the challenge of saving more money.

10. Every dollar saved puts me closer to financial freedom.

11. I have the ability to spend money on the things that matter to me most.

12. I am happy when I spend my money responsibly.

13. I am more than my debt.

14. My debt doesn't control me.

15. I am committed to eliminating all debts that don't serve me from my life.

16. I spend money on what matters to me, not what matters to the Jones.

17. Making choices to build wealth today can allow me to build the life I desire.

18. I have the ability to build a base of financial literacy.

19. I am excited to keep my finances on the right path.

20. I deserve a prosperous life.

21. Money is a tool that can change my life for the better.

22. I control money, money doesn't control me.

23. Money flows to me freely as I move through this world.

24. I can use money to create a better life.

25. My finances don't scare me because I have a plan.

26. I am worthy of a solid financial foundation.

27. Money can expand the opportunities of my life.

28. Negative emotions about money don't serve my financial goals.

29. I am a very capable person that can tackle all money obstacles.

30. More money in my bank account doesn't make me a bad person.

31. I am not poor; I am on the path to a wealthy life.

32. I can become financially free.

33. I have the power to be a financially successful person.

34. I have the power to improve my relationship with money.

35. I can find the positive in my money situation.

36. Through thoughtful generosity, more money will flow back to me.

37. My life is full of wealth beyond money.

38. I believe in my ability to use the money that comes into my life to meet my financial goals.

39. It is within my power to create a successful financial future.

40. With hard work and creativity, I can build the financial picture that I desire.

Affirmations For Parents & Parents-To-Be

Success is not just about what you accomplish in life; it's about what you inspire others to do.

Unknown

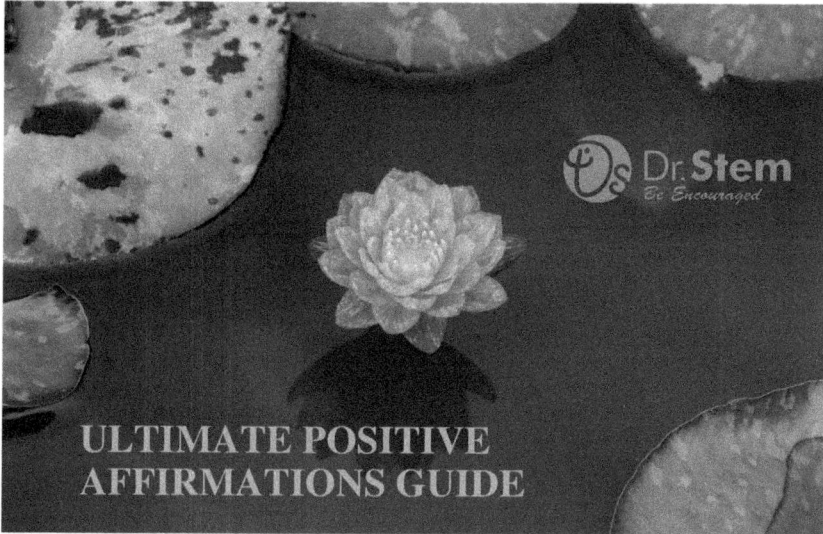

ULTIMATE POSITIVE
AFFIRMATIONS GUIDE

1. My income can exceed my expenses.

2. Money is an abundant resource that I can earn.

3. My income has unlimited potential and money constantly flows to me with ease

4. I accept the flow of money from multiple sources.

5. My hard work will bring me money.

6. I can leverage my skills to bring in more money at any time.

7. I believe in my ability to earn more money.

8. There are countless opportunities to make more money in my life.

9. I deserve the opportunity to negotiate my salary

10. I deserve to be paid a fair wage for my skills and time.

11. My job provides the opportunity to work towards my financial goals.

12. I can use money to change the world for the better.

13. I have enough money to freely enjoy my day-to-day life.

14. I will attain all the riches that I desire with time.

15. I am on my way to becoming wealthy

16. I am a successful person.

17. I am confident in everything that I do.

18. I am doing the best I can.

19. I choose to be happy.

20. I am in perfect health.

21. I am resilient; I will get through this difficult time.

22. I believe in myself.

23. I accept myself.

24. I love myself.

25. I don't judge myself.

26. I don't compare myself to others.

If you
DON'T FIND A WAY TO MAKE MONEY WHILE YOU SLEEP, YOU WILL WORK UNTIL YOU DIE

Dr. Stem
Be Encouraged

Affirmations For Overcoming Bad Days, Stress & Adversity

If you care about what you do and work hard at it, there isn't anything you can't do if you want to.

Jim Henson

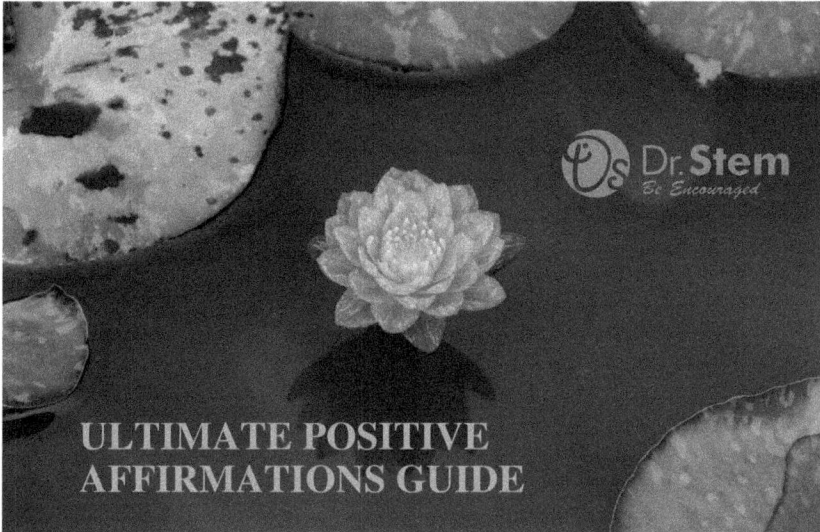

ULTIMATE POSITIVE
AFFIRMATIONS GUIDE

1. I release all negative emotions from the day.

2. I let go of any stress and anxiety from today.

3. I will learn what I need to from today which will make me a stronger person.

4. I know that life is not meant to be easy.

5. Tomorrow is a brand-new day.

6. I release all negativity from my life.

7. I am filled with joy and ease right now.

8. I don't have to have this all solved today.

9. I am doing what I can with the knowledge and skills I have to survive this.

5. When I have done all, I know how to do, I choose to let my mind rest.

6. I welcome fear as a sign to be careful but choose to let go of it when it no longer serves me.

7. I am doing the best I can, and thus choose to release myself from guilt and shame.

8. I am slowly becoming the kind of person who can survive this storm.

9. When circumstances change, I will feel all the more grateful for what I have.

10. I am not a failure, but a survivor. I am daily in the process of surviving.

11. My commitment to showing up tomorrow overshadows the mistakes I have made.

12. I am holding on in the dark to what I know to be true in the light, in better times.

13. I am not the only one to have faced this sort of trauma, and I will not be the last.

14. I am flexible and can adapt when life doesn't go according to plan.

15. Courage does not mean having no fear of danger but facing the danger despite that fear.

16. Life's problems are not solved by perfect people, but by those who show up. I am someone who shows up.

17. I know when to persevere along a path and when to let go and change course.

18. I don't have to go this road alone. I have, or can find, people in my life and examples to support and inspire me.

19. I am worthy of love and my life is meaningful despite my losses.

20. Life is full of constant change. My pain, though very real, will not be as acute forever.

21. This is just one chapter in my life's story.

Affirmations For The **Go-Getter** in You; for Setting Goals and Finishing Projects

Strength does not come from physical capacity. It comes from a spirit with indomitable will.

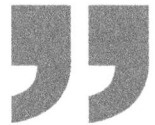

— Mahatma Gandi

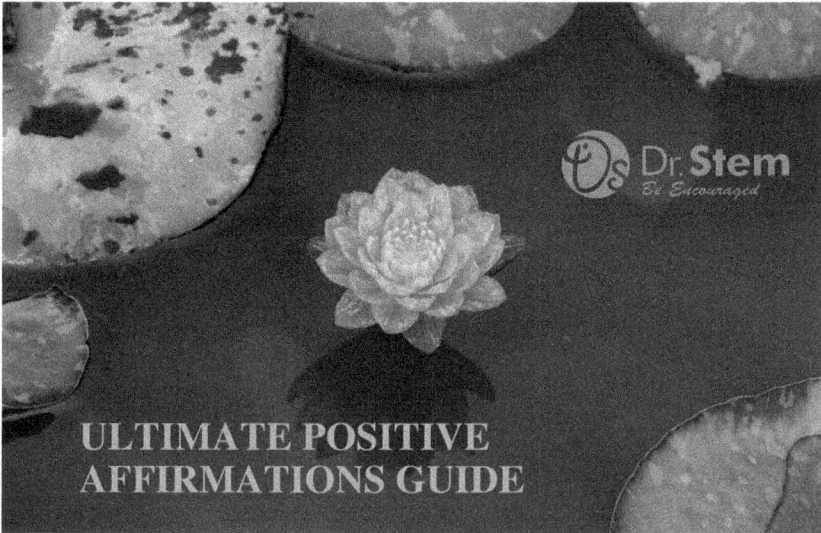

ULTIMATE POSITIVE
AFFIRMATIONS GUIDE

1. I am a do-er. I will take action and get things accomplished.

2. I find the work I need to do to be fascinating.

3. For today, I am truly attentive on my work.

4. I will be observant and attentive throughout my entire day.

5. I can focus and concentrate at will.

6. I release negativity. Instead, I focus on positivity and productivity!

7. I have clarity and energy.

8. I am committed to being focus on my goal. I am worth it.

9. I concentrate all my efforts on the things I want to accomplish in life.

10. I can work my way into the flow state whenever I wish.

11. I am calm and focused in all that I do.

12. I will face difficult situations with grace and courage. I will find solutions in these difficult times.

13. I will work with abundant enthusiasm and confidence.

14. I will live my life as the exciting adventure that it is.

15. I will follow the beat of my inner drummer. I will be myself; not what others want me to be.

16. Today I will take a big step toward reaching my goals.

17. All resistance achieving my goal has vanished.

18. I know where I am going. I only need to supply the action to get there.

19. My mind is energized, clear and focused on the process of my goals.

20. I free myself from the doubt and pessimism that keep me from achieving my goals.

21. I clearly visualize the attainment of my goals.

22. Giving up is easy. I will continue striving for my goals.

23. I clearly see the obstacles to keep me from achieving my goals I move over, under, through or around them.

24. My planning, action and hard work will translate to the achievement of my desires.

25. My daily goals will ensure I reach my long-term goals.

26. I live in the present, never dwelling on the past, and take action to ensure a wonderful future.

27. I will turn my dreams into goals. I will turn my goals into steps. I will turn my steps into actions. I will complete an action every day.

28. I will face my fears head on. I will learn from them.

29. I am willing to explore new and uncharted territory

Affirmations To
Stop Procrastinating

Obsessed is just a word the lady use to describe the dedicated.

— Russell Warren

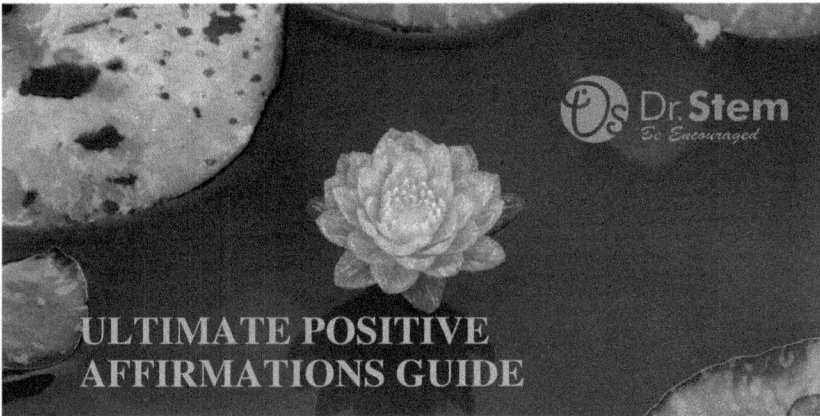

ULTIMATE POSITIVE
AFFIRMATIONS GUIDE

1. I get things done fast.

2. I never put things off.

3. I am a doer.

4. I act quickly.

5. I am motivated to finish my tasks.

6. I have the willpower to do my assignments.

7. I am a proactive person.

8. I finish my projects effortlessly.

9. I love taking action.

10. Nothing will stand in my way of accomplishing my tasks.

11. No excuses. Just results.

12. Every day I am moving my life forward.

13. I am determined to get everything done.

Affirmations For
Self - Determination

Shallow men believe in luck. Strong men believe in cause and effect through deliberate actions.

—————————— Ralph Waldo Emerson

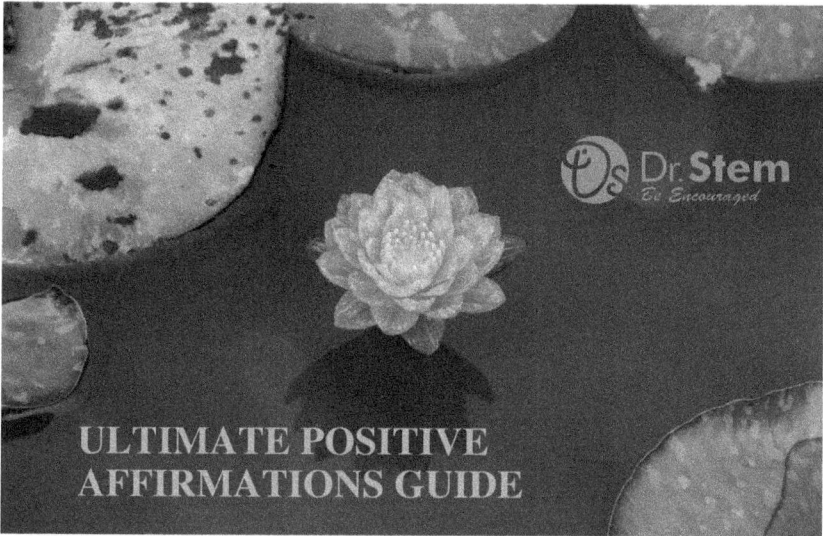

ULTIMATE POSITIVE
AFFIRMATIONS GUIDE

"I AM" Affirmations

1. I am enough

2. I am worthy

3. I am capable

4. I am confident

5. I am strong

6. I am courageous

7. I am talented

8. I am resilient

9. I am confident in myself and my actions

10. I am wanted

11. I am safe

12. I am loved

13. I am brave

14. I am beautiful

15. I am funny

16. I am kind

17. I am learning to love myself

18. I am learning to believe in myself

19. I am learning my worth

20. I am learning to accept myself

21. I am learning to forgive myself

22. I am learning to believe in my strength

23. I am learning to love myself

"I BELIEVE" Affirmations

1. I believe in myself

2. I believe in my abilities

3. I believe in my dreams

4. I believe in my passions

5. I believe good things are coming

6. I believe I am worthy

7. I believe I am worthy of good things

8. I believe I am worthy of love

9. I believe I am enough

"I ACCEPT" Affirmations

1. I accept myself as I am

2. I accept my flaws

3. I accept my past

4. I accept my wrongdoings

5. I accept my feelings

6. I accept my power

7. I accept my strength

8. I accept my vulnerability

9. I accept love from myself and others

10. I accept kindness from myself and others

11. I accept change

"I CAN" Affirmations

1. I can do hard things

2. I can accomplish great things

3. I can accomplish my dreams and goals

4. I can provide for my family

5. I can be true to myself

6. I can learn and grow

7. I can create the life of my dreams

8. I can do anything I set my mind to

9. I can overcome obstacles

10. I can get through this

11. I can come out of this stronger

12. I can come out of this smarter

13. I can make a difference in the world

with

BRAVE wings SHE flies

Dr. Stem
Be Encouraged

Affirmations For Becoming The Best Version of Yourself & Allowing Your Light To Shine

To succeed in life, you need two things; ignorance and confidence.

Mark Twain

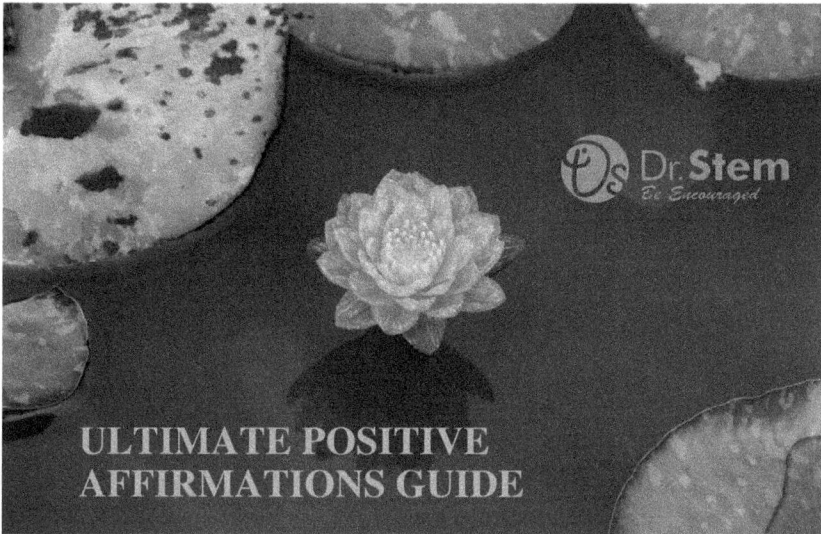

**ULTIMATE POSITIVE
AFFIRMATIONS GUIDE**

1. I am aware of my gift to the world and share it freely.

2. I am compassionate with others and myself.

3. I am a positive being, aware of my potential.

4. There are no blocks I cannot overcome.

5. I love to meet other people and make new friends.

6. I am my best source of motivation.

7. Challenges are opportunities to grow and improve.

8. I attract positive people into my life.

9. I make a difference by showing up every day and doing my best.

10. I am becoming a better version of myself one day at a time.

11. I am worthy of having what I want.

12. I am grateful for my journey and its lessons.

13. I accept compliments easily.

14. Everything is possible.

15. I am creative and open to new solutions.

16. I choose to embrace the mystery of life.

17. I already have what I need.

18. What I want is already here or on its way.

19. I appreciate all that I have.

20. I allow everything to be as it is.

21. I enjoy going with the flow.

22. The more I let go, the better I feel.

23. I live from a place of abundance.

24. I release anything that doesn't serve me.

25. I believe in my abilities and express my true self with ease.

26. All I need is within me.

27. I am stronger than I seem.

28. I am braver than I think.

29. I have unshakable faith.

30. Miracles are taking place in my life.

31. I am worthy. I am loved. I am enough.

32. I am whole just as I am.

33. I give myself unconditional love!

34. I feel great about who I am.

35. My life is amazing!

36. I have unlimited power.

37. I believe in myself and my power.

38. Others love me for who I am.

39. I treat myself with respect and honor.

40. People treat me with respect.

41. I view myself through kind eyes.

42. I feel comfortable speaking my mind.

43. I love to share my ideas and thoughts.

44. I have unique and special ideas to share with the world.

45. I am grateful for the amazing, wonderful things in my life!

46. I deserve everything I desire.

47. My life is rewarding and filled with joy.

48. I am blessed.

49. My life is full of adventure and incredible experiences.

50. I accept and embrace myself for who I am.

51. I love who I am inside and out.

52. I am creative and flexible, and I go with the flow of life.

53. I expect the best for myself!

54. My life is abundant.

55. The Universe is generous with health, joy, and abundance!

56. I learn and grow every day.

57. I adapt and change to my circumstances. I flow like a river.

58. I am worthy of all the abundance, love, and amazing experiences I want.

59. Others look up to me.

60. I feel joyful to look at how far I've come.

61. I grow and become a better version of myself every day!

62. I am confident and intelligent.

63. I am beautiful.

64. I love myself more and more each passing day.

65. I appreciate myself.

66. I give praise to myself and to others naturally and effortlessly!

67. I naturally feel good about myself!

68. I forgive myself.

69. I easily forgive others.

70. I do my best every day.

71. I am optimistic and positive!

72. I am courageous and outgoing!

73. I fearlessly follow my dreams!

74. I am capable of achieving everything I want.

75. Others value my skills and knowledge.

76. I contribute my ideas and thoughts easily.

77. My life is a blessing.

78. I am loved.

79. I love myself. I accept myself. I forgive myself.

80. I know myself and I honor my boundaries.

81. I radiate self-confidence!

82. I have great potential that I tap into every day!

83. I can achieve anything I put my mind to.

84. I make a difference in the world

85. I believe in myself and my dreams

86. I am doing my best

87. I love myself for who I am (or I am working on loving myself for all that I am)

88. I am in charge of my happiness and do not let it be dependent on others

89. I accept my past, present, and future self

90. I am worthy of love

91. I am worthy of good things

IF YOU WANT TO FLY. YOU HAVE TO GIVE UP THE THINGS THAT WEIGH YOU DOWN.

Dr. Stem
Be Encouraged

Conclusion:
Can Affirmations Change
Negative Thoughts?

Everyone wants to ride the train, but not everyone wants to lay the tracks.

— Anonymous

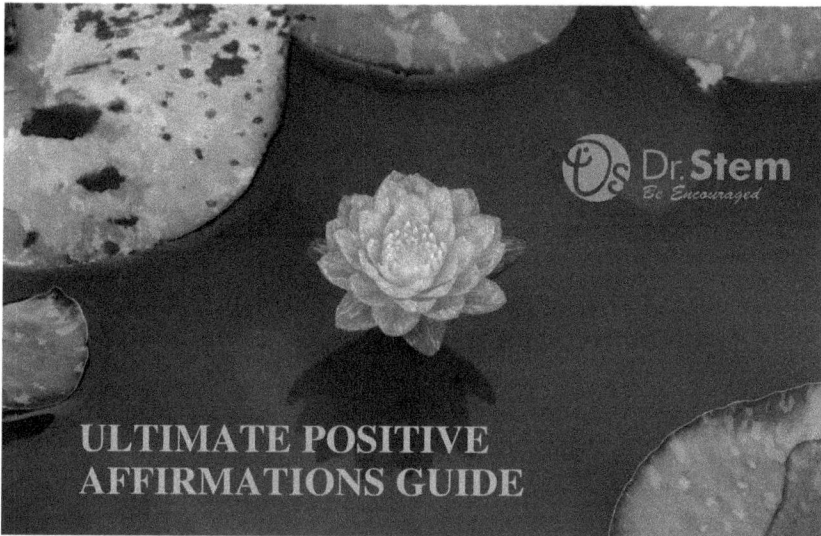

ULTIMATE POSITIVE AFFIRMATIONS GUIDE

In conclusion let me address this key question.

Affirmations, overall as we discussed earlier influence your thinking by addressing what's going on in your head right now.

Affirmations aren't about fixing the past or securing the future.

Affirmations address the negative thinking that's holding you back in the present.

Affirmations challenge the negative thinking and introduce full complete focus on the present, the here and now.

Affirmations gives you a chance to see each situation, moment in a different way that is more solution focuses, which means there are many ways every outcome could turn out: win-win, win-lose, stand to understand and be understand or resort to being ok without understanding or understood.

Affirmations are positive truths you can repeat throughout the day to forge new neutral pathways and create a new and improved mindset, peacefulness, less stress, and attitude.

Decide that reading and repeating affirming words will be part of your daily life for the rest of your life.

Just like taking your daily vitamin or doing your workout, using affirmations can protect your mental and physical health and train your brain to focus on gratitude, success, and positivity.

And who doesn't want that?

Wishing you a life filled with peace, joy, happiness, health and yes wealth.

Dr. **Stem**
Be Encouraged

BE YOU
BE FREE
BE FEARLESS

Dr. Stem
Be Encouraged

Congratulations on purchasing this to journaling, an easy guide to help you pick a question and write. I have no doubt this will change your life. Make this a lifelong project of writing about your life.

Don't forget to check out the FOUR Lesson Course on Journaling to help you with the step by step guide to journaling titled:

The Ultimate Freedom Journaling Course on my website www.drstemmie.com that goes hand in hand with this guide.

DrStem Books and eBooks

eBOOKs now available on www.drstemmie.com under **"Empowerment Books"** tab.

These Books are available on **AMAZON** and Book Stores near you.

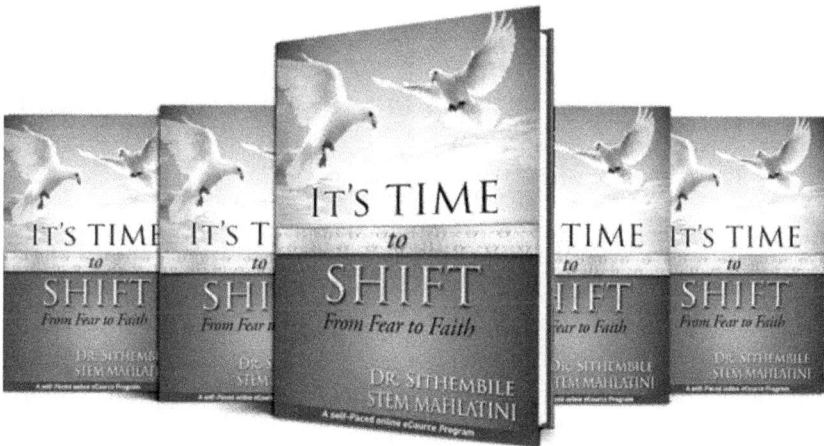

ABOUT THE EMPOWERMENT ACADEMY

The Empowerment Academy is a platform where women can have full access to life, career and business coaching, digital programs, eBooks, and tools for success in life, career and business with membership or individual bookings.

Corporations and Organizations can enjoy providing their employees with state-of-the-art wellness trainings, workshops, and digital programs. Trainings cover mental and health wellness, leaderships -Management skills, mindfulness, time management, organizational skills and more.

The Self-Care Workshops lift women up. The workshops are geared towards letting women know that they can be more, and each workshop provides them with the tools and the support to become more.

The Empowerment Academy provides all round real empowerment: with deep insight programs that address childhood issues, fears, mindfulness, stress management and success programs, with emphasis on an internal and positive change in each woman, so that she can find her passion, and purpose and change her life on her own terms.

Dr. Stem
Be Encouraged

THERE ARE TWO WOLVES INSIDE EACH OF US

ONE IS EVIL	ONE IS GOOD
ANGER	JOY
ENVY	PEACE
SORROW	HOPE
REGRET	SERENITY
GREED	LOVE
ARROGANCE	HUMILITY
SELF-PITY	KINDNESS
GUILT	PATIENCE
RESENTMENT	BENEVOLANCE
INFERIORITY	EMPATHY
DECEPTION	GENEROSITY
FALSE PRIDE	TRUTH
SUPERIORITY	COMPASSION
AND EGO	AND FAITH

Whichever WOLF wins is the one
YOU feed most.

Dr Stem (Sithembile Mahlatini, EdD, LCSW) Zimbabwe, Africa is an Employee Assistant Professional, Transitions Trainer, Speaker, Television & Radio Personality, Author and Licensed psychotherapist.

She is a Certified John Maxwell Leadership Trainer/Speaker, Certified Life- Career Coach, Passion test Facilitator and Josh Shipp Certified Youth Speaker.

As an author of 35 books she is Focused on three things: To Inspire, Influence and Impact.

Her joy is in helping you live a stress free lives and easily manifest wealth and health.

Email drstem14@gmail.com

People call Dr.Stem when they need to improve personal, professional, or business performance. Typically this is where she helps:

Help for individuals to;

- Get clear on their business and life goals
- Elevate their presents in their niche
- Connect More and Communicate Better in their relationships
- Manage Stress
- Manage the stress related to Career, Business, and relationship Decisions

Dr.Stem provides individual business coaching as well conduct workshops and training on the following:

- Stress Management and Leadership Trainings.
- Mindfulness Training.
- Relationship management.
- Managing change
- Balancing Work, Business and Life

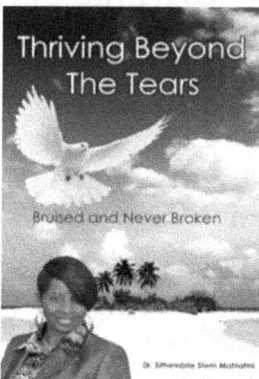

Read my Memoir easy download on my website or book on amazon or any bookstore near you.

E- Book Now available on www.drstemmie.com under Empowerment Books

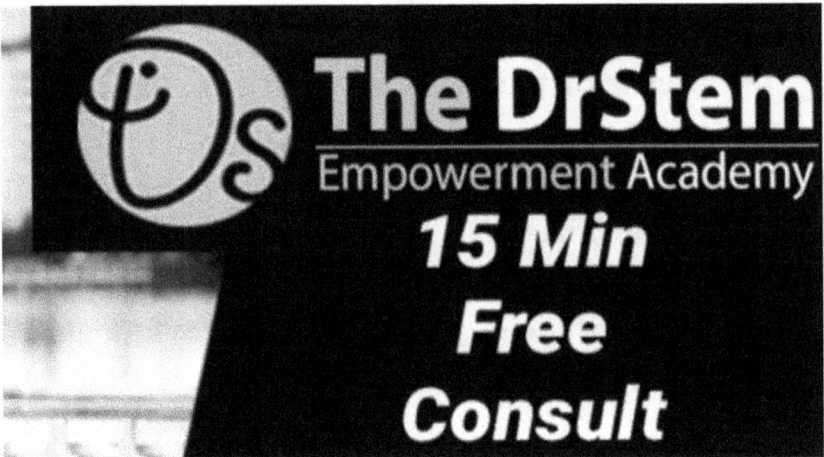

More Self Care Resources

Visit Our website at: www.drstemmie.com

Self-Care Workshops Relaxation

Join Our Memberships to Attend Workshops For Free or Pay as You Go for each Workshop.

For more information, including workshop topics and dates: Visit www.drstemmie.com

For one-on-one stress management coaching and counseling, please call 781 (254-1602) or email drstem14@gmail.com for more information.

Digital Courses and E Books

Visit our website www.drstemmie.com and go to Digital Courses Tab:
https://www.drstemmie.com/empowermentebooks

or the Parent TeenTab:
https://www.drstemmie.com/parentsteensebooks

268

NOTES:

DR. STEM SITHEMBILE MAHLATINI

www.drstemmie.com

www.ingramcontent.com/pod-product-compliance
Lightning Source LLC
Chambersburg PA
CBHW051905090426
42811CB00003B/469